LYNN BEDFORD H

CREATIV
COOKING
in colour

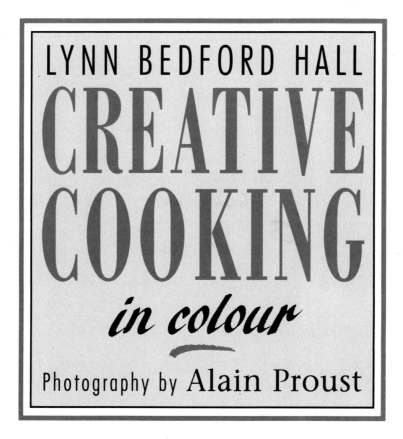

LYNN BEDFORD HALL

CREATIVE COOKING
in colour

Photography by Alain Proust

NEW HOLLAND

First published in the UK in 1993 by
New Holland (Publishers) Ltd
37 Connaught Street, London W2 2AZ

ISBN 1 85368 249 7
Editor: Inge du Plessis
Cover designer: Janice Evans
Designers: Janice Evans and Joan Sutton
Assistant designer: Lellyn Creamer
Front cover photographer: Malcolm Dare
Photographer: Alain Proust
Stylists: Macushla Falkiner, Georgia Shubitz and Marine Williams
Food preparation: Ivy Tingwe
Phototypeset by Struik DTP
Reproduction by Unifoto (Pty) Ltd
Printed and bound in Hong Kong by South China Printing Co. Ltd

CONTENTS

INTRODUCTION

The recipes in this book are not basic, but neither can they be classed as haute cuisine – no caviar, truffles, veal stock or hearts of lamb. There isn't even one Hollandaise or Béarnaise Sauce lurking between the pages. The recipes, rather, are sandwiched somewhere inbetween – like a filling of smoked salmon between slices of plain brown bread. The simpler ones should add a bit of glitz to family meals, while others, slightly more sophisticated, will add glamour to party fare. This makes it a book for cooks on all levels, with the accent lying on creative meals which are visually tempting and enticingly flavoured.

A glance at the index will, I hope, set the taste-buds tingling. Much use has been made of herbs and spices. Salads occupy an important slot, especially as trendy starters, and many dishes are linked to the fragrant cuisines of the East, or have a colourful and robust Mediterranean touch. Many of the recipes have been devised with an eye to current trend-setting foods and ingredients on both the local and international scenes.

And if that sounds a little heavy, let me hasten to add that the idea remains to inspire, not intimidate. Rules are often bent to make the average cook's life easier. I often thicken sauces instead of spending time reducing them; I like to pre-prepare whenever possible; and I prefer to use my oven instead of standing watch over the cooker. Although the desserts are mostly upmarket and indulgent, quick dishes and budget ingredients have not been neglected, with vegetables and fruit playing an important role in all sections.

If the culinary fairy should grant me three wishes, these are they: may some of these recipes become family favourites; may others prove your prowess as a hostess and delight your guests; and may the whole collection add a new dimension to the phrase 'food with flair'.

Lynn Bedford Hall

SMOKED SALMON SPREAD

An expensive cocktail snack, but what a joy when time is limited. It takes but a few minutes to whip up in a food processor, and is then left to firm up in the refrigerator. At the witching hour, spread it thickly on fingers or circles of wholewheat bread, grind plenty of black pepper over the tops, pass with the drinks – you won't have any leftovers.

day-old wholemeal bread
milled black pepper
a few capers (optional)
fronds of dill or nasturtium
  leaves for garnish

SPREAD
125–150 g (4–5 oz) smoked
  salmon slices or off-cuts
250 g (9 oz) curd cheese
25 ml (5 tsp) lemon juice
pinch each of salt and sugar
50 g (2 oz) very soft butter
a few drops of Tabasco sauce

To make spread, place all ingredients in a food processor fitted with grinding blade and process until smooth. Turn into a container and chill for a few hours.

To assemble snacks, slice bread medium-thin – if you slice it too daintily the fingers will bend in half as guests help themselves, and drop onto the carpet. Cut off side crusts. Spread slices thickly with salmon spread. Grind pepper over, then cut each slice into three fingers. (Alternatively, cut small circles from each crustless slice, using a small scone cutter – this will take a little longer, but the snacks will look smarter.)

Arrange snacks on a pretty plate. Garnish each finger or round with one or two capers, if using, and the plate with fronds of dill or nasturtium leaves.
Serves 12.

MUSHROOM CROSTINI

These crisp bread rounds with a delectable topping make the perfect snack. The mushroom mixture may be made the day before and refrigerated, the bread cut and crisped in advance. Simply assemble, refrigerate, and bake when needed.

12–16 slices slightly stale,
  white or plain brown bread
45 ml (3 tbsp) sunflower oil
  and 15 g (½ oz) butter,
  melted together
45 g (1½ oz) butter
250 g (9 oz) white or brown
  mushrooms, wiped and
  very finely chopped
45 ml (3 tbsp) plain flour
250 ml (8 fl oz) milk
6 spring onions, finely
  chopped
1.25 ml (¼ tsp) dried oregano
salt and milled black pepper
8 black olives, slivered
grated Parmesan cheese

Slice crusts off bread and stamp out rounds using a 5 cm (2 in) scone cutter. Place on a baking tray and brush both sides with the melted oil and butter. Bake at 180 °C (350 °F, gas 4) for 10–12 minutes, until golden brown and crisp, turning once. Cool.

Melt 45 g (1½ oz) butter in a small saucepan, add mushrooms and toss over low heat until soft and all liquid has evaporated. Sprinkle in flour, and when absorbed, slowly add milk. Bring to the boil and stir until very thick. Remove from hob and add spring onions, oregano and seasoning to taste. (If preparing in advance, cool, cover and refrigerate at this stage.)

To bake, spread mushroom mixture thickly on each round of bread, top with olives and sprinkle with Parmesan. Bake at 200 °C (400 °F, gas 6) for 12–15 minutes, until piping hot. Serve immediately.
Makes about 36.

HERBY RICOTTA AND POPPY SEED PÂTÉ

Even with the addition of butter, Ricotta lends itself well to shaping as it is a fairly dry and firm cheese. Pat into a thick sausage or log shape, roll in nuts or chives and serve on a cheese board, as an alternative to dessert.

300 g (11 oz) Ricotta cheese
salt and milled black pepper
60 g (2 oz) soft butter
10 ml (2 tsp) chopped basil
20 ml (4 tsp) chopped parsley
3–4 slim spring onions, chopped
10 ml (2 tsp) poppy seeds
coarsely crushed walnuts or
    chopped chives to coat

Cream all ingredients, except walnuts or chives, together. Shape pâté into a roll, wrap in greaseproof paper, and chill until firm.

Unwrap and roll in crushed walnuts or chopped chives before serving.
Serves 4–6.

HINT
The pâté may also be spooned into a small china bowl and sprinkled with walnuts or chives. Serve as a spread with savoury biscuits.

MUSHROOMS WITH CAMEMBERT AND ALMONDS

May be served hot as a starter, or, because they are poised on crisp bread rounds, these succulent mushrooms may also be served as a snack with drinks. In this case use medium rather than large mushrooms, and allow to cool slightly before passing round. This dish may be completely assembled in advance and grilled before serving.

8 slices of white or plain
    brown bread
45 ml (3 tbsp) sunflower oil
    and 20 g (¾ oz) butter,
    melted together
8 large brown mushrooms,
    wiped
25 ml (5 tsp) sunflower oil
half a bunch of spring onions,
    chopped
8 large spinach leaves, ribs
    removed and finely shredded
salt and milled black pepper
slivered almonds
a few thin slices Camembert*

Using a 7.5 cm (3 in) scone cutter, cut each slice of bread into a circle. Brush both sides of each circle with melted oil and butter. Place on baking tray and bake at 180 °C (350 °F, gas 4) for about 15 minutes, until golden-brown and crisp, turning once. Set aside.

Cut off mushroom stems and scoop out a little of the centre of each cap. Chop stems and centres finely, and set aside.

Brush mushroom caps on both sides with extra oil, or remaining melted oil and butter, and bake at 180 °C (350 °F, gas 4) for about 5 minutes, until just starting to soften. Season with pepper, and cool.

Heat oil in a small saucepan, add onions and mushroom trimmings, and fry until softened. Add spinach and toss until wilted. Season lightly and cool.

To assemble, divide spinach mixture equally between mushroom caps. Tuck in almonds, here and there, and top generously with cheese. Place each mushroom on a circle of crisp bread. (If preparing in advance, arrange in fridge-to-oven dish at this stage, and chill.)

To serve, pre-heat grill, place mushrooms well below heat, and grill for 4–5 minutes until bubbling, and cheese is melted and golden brown.
Serves 4 as a starter.

* Use mozzarella if preferred.

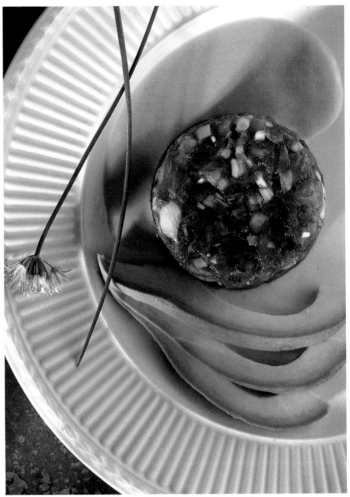

AVOCADO MOUSSE WITH SMOKED SALMON

Here are two stylish ways of presenting a simple avocado mousse: once set, it may either be rolled up in salmon slices like thin crêpes, or it may be used to fill individual ramekins lined with slices of smoked salmon. The latter is the more economical method of the two, as, instead of lining the base and sides of the ramekin, a round of salmon, or a circle of strips, may simply be nestled on the base of each. This upmarket starter is very easy to make, and the accompaniments are minimal – don't be tempted to tart it up with any ubiquitous pools of sauce.

As the flavours are so delicate, the only additions should be a twist of lemon, a wafer of melba toast, and a pepper mill. It is important to use a light, homemade chicken stock – a stock cube simply will not do.

15 ml (1 tbsp) gelatine
125 ml (4 fl oz) chicken stock
2 large or 3 medium, firm, ripe
    avocados (about 675 g
    (1 1/2 lb)), peeled and stoned
pinch of salt
a few drops of Tabasco sauce
25 ml (5 tsp) lemon juice
45 ml (3 tbsp) thick
    mayonnaise
45 ml (3 tbsp) thick, cultured
    sour cream or crème fraîche
smoked salmon slices, at
    least 150 g (5 oz)

Sponge gelatine in stock and dissolve over low heat. Using a silver fork, mash avocados with salt, Tabasco and lemon juice. Slowly stir in dissolved gelatine, then add mayonnaise and soured cream or crème fraîche; whisk until smooth. Check seasoning. Mixture should be thick enough to use almost at once, but on a hot day you might have to chill it slightly.

Now either spoon mousse onto salmon slices, roll up, arrange two on each serving plate, cover and chill until needed, or rinse 10 small ramekins (for easy unmoulding) and line base, or sides and base, with salmon slices and fill with mousse. Press mousse down with back of a spoon, cover and chill until firm. To unmould, run a knife round edges and turn onto serving plates. Serve on the same day mousse is made.
Makes about 12 rolls, or fills 10 small ramekins.

TOMATOES EN GELÉE

Add a splash of drama to a ladies' luncheon with this stunning starter.

500 g (18 oz) firm, ripe
    tomatoes, skinned, seeded
    and chopped
4 slim spring onions, finely
    chopped
a few pinches each of salt,
    black pepper and sugar
45 ml (3 tbsp) finely chopped
    parsley
400 ml (14 fl oz) canned pure
    tomato juice (not tomato
    cocktail)
15 ml (1 tbsp) gelatine
20 ml (4 tsp) medium-dry
    sherry
a few drops of Worcestershire
    sauce
thinly sliced avocado and
    milled black pepper

YELLOW PEPPER DRESSING
250 g (9 oz) yellow peppers,
    cored, seeded and roughly
    chopped
100 ml (3 1/2 fl oz) water
1 pickling onion, chopped
1 clove garlic, halved
2.5 ml (1/2 tsp) ground cumin
2.5 ml (1/2 tsp) turmeric
1.25 ml 1/4 tsp) salt
2.5 ml (1/2 tsp) sugar
10 ml (2 tsp) lemon juice
about 30 ml (2 tbsp) thick
    mayonnaise

Divide tomatoes, spring onions, seasoning and parsley between eight ramekins, mixing lightly. Pour tomato juice into small saucepan, sprinkle on the gelatine, then stir over low heat just until gelatine has dissolved – do not boil. Remove from heat, stir in sherry and Worcestershire sauce, and pour into ramekins, dividing equally. Cool, then chill for several hours until set.

To make dressing, place all the ingredients, except lemon juice and mayonnaise, in a small saucepan, bring to the boil, then cover and simmer gently until peppers are soft. You might have to add a little more water to prevent scorching, but end result should be juicy and thick, not watery.

Cool mixture briefly, add lemon juice, then purée in a blender until absolutely smooth. Spoon into a container, stir in enough mayonnaise to give a sauce-like consistency, cover and chill.

To serve, run a flat-bladed knife round sides of ramekins and invert onto individual plates. Flank with dressing on one side and avocado slices on the other. Dust with pepper, and serve. **Serves 8.**

SALAD WITH NUTS, HERBS AND BLUE CHEESE DRESSING

A top favourite in the line of composed starter salads. Serve with wedges of instant Garlic and Herb Pittas (see hint). The salad leaves used may be altered with regard to quantity. I have measured these in a measuring jug to act as a guide.

1 red lettuce, roughly torn (about 2 litres (3 ½ pints))
1 iceberg lettuce, roughly torn (about 2 litres (3 ½ pints))
100 ml (7 tbsp) chopped chives shredded spinach leaves (about 1 litre (1 ¾ pints))
100 ml (7 tbsp) chopped basil leaves
100 ml (7 tbsp) chopped borage leaves
75–100 g (2 ½–3 ½ oz) chopped, toasted walnuts or pecan nuts
250 g (9 oz) white mushrooms, wiped and thinly sliced
20 ml (4 tsp) walnut or sunflower oil
sliced avocado for garnish

DRESSING
1 small clove garlic, peeled
25 ml (5 tsp) tarragon vinegar
25 ml (5 tsp) lemon juice
250–300 ml (8–10 fl oz) sunflower oil
a few sprigs parsley
about 60 g (2 oz) blue cheese, diced
2.5 ml (½ tsp) Worcestershire sauce
2.5 ml (½ tsp) sugar
200 ml (7 fl oz) thick Bulgarian yoghurt (optional)*

Place all dressing ingredients, except yoghurt, in blender goblet and blend until smooth and creamy. Tip into a bowl and stir in the yoghurt, if using.

Place all salad ingredients, except oil and avocado slices, in a large bowl and toss – it's easiest if you simply use your hands. Add oil, and toss. Add just enough dressing to moisten and flavour, and toss again. Arrange on serving plates, and garnish with avocado.
Serves 10.

* The addition of Bulgarian yoghurt is a good way of thinning down and extending a rich dressing, and is especially recommended if your salad includes mushrooms.

HINT
For instant Garlic and Herb Pittas, use bought pitta breads, brush with garlic oil, sprinkle with dried oregano and heat in a moderate oven for 10 minutes.

ASPARAGUS

When purchasing fresh asparagus, choose fairly slender green stalks with the tips still tightly closed, buy them not more than one day in advance and keep them refrigerated.

If they are young, the only pre-preparation necessary is a gentle rinsing, and a snapping off of the tips at the base. With slender, green asparagus they will snap off in just the right place, about 2.5 cm (1 in) from the ends. Larger asparagus may have to have the stalks shaved with a vegetable peeler.

To cook, simply place stalks in a single layer in a wide-based, shallow saucepan with a little boiling, salted water, and cook briefly, uncovered, until tender-crisp. Once cooked, refresh them under cold water or plunge them into iced water to set the colour. Drain on paper towels and use as required.

ASPARAGUS WITH ORANGE-MUSTARD DRESSING

Fresh asparagus makes the perfect choice for an elegant and popular starter, and although good hot, it is so much more convenient served cold. The following dressing will lift each spear to new heights.

48–60 young, green asparagus spears, cooked (see box alongside) and chilled

DRESSING
1 whole egg and 1 yolk
45 ml (3 tbsp) fresh orange juice
2.5 ml (¹/₂ tsp) finely grated orange rind
1.25 ml (¹/₄ tsp) salt
10 ml (2 tsp) pale, thin honey
250 ml (8 fl oz) sunflower oil
15 ml (1 tbsp) wholegrain mustard
5 ml (1 tsp) brandy

To make dressing, place whole egg and yolk, orange juice and rind, salt and honey in a blender goblet and blend until thoroughly combined. Very slowly, while blending, dribble in oil. By the time all the oil has been used, mixture will have emulsified to a medium-thick consistency. Spoon into a container, stir in mustard and brandy, and chill for several hours to thicken mixture and ripen flavour.

Arrange about six cooked and chilled asparagus spears (depending on size) on each plate, and spoon a generous dollop of dressing across middle. Garnish with a nasturtium flower to tie in with the summery mood. **Serves 8–10.**

HINT
To cut the richness of the dressing, gently fold in some thick Bulgarian yoghurt – 1 part yoghurt to 3 parts dressing is a good ratio.

PEARS WITH ROCKET AND SAVOURY SABAYON

A gourmet starter with which to stun your guests: poached pears, a trend-setting herb, and a dream of a dressing. Normally I do not like to serve starters rich with eggs and cream, as the rest of the courses then need to be chosen with a careful eye to the possibility of over-indulgence, thereby cancelling creamy casseroles and wanton desserts. But this sauce is so special, and is used in such modest quantities, that I am happy to make an exception. Do not use canned pears for this dish – they are too sweet – so if pears are out of season, try the sabayon with asparagus or poached leeks. Not difficult to make, it is started off in a blender for convenience. The only pitfall is allowing it to scramble, but if you follow the instructions you should not have a problem.

6 medium, not-quite-ripe,
  perfectly shaped Bon
  Chrétien pears
lemon juice and sugar
fresh rocket leaves for garnish

SAVOURY SABAYON
2 eggs
10 ml (2 tsp) caster sugar
25 ml (5 tsp) tarragon wine
  vinegar
2.5 ml (½ tsp) dried tarragon
5 ml (1 tsp) mustard powder
6 sage leaves
1.25 ml (¼ tsp) salt
5 ml (1 tsp) cornflour
125 ml (4 fl oz) whipping
  cream

Peel, halve and core pears, then place, rounded sides up, in a large frying pan. Add a little water and sprinkle each pear half with 5 ml (1 tsp) lemon juice and 2.5 ml (½ tsp) sugar. Cover frying pan and poach gently until just soft. Cool, remove pears from liquid, cover and chill until ready to serve.

To make savoury sabayon, place all ingredients, except cream, in a blender and blend well. Transfer to top of a small double boiler and whisk, using a balloon whisk, over simmering water, until mixture thickens, then stir constantly with a wooden spoon until cooked and creamy. Do not let bottom of upper pan rest in hot water, or mixture will scramble. Spoon into a container, and chill. Whip and fold in cream just before serving.

To serve, place one pear half on each plate. Flank with two to three rocket leaves, and coat each pear with a little dressing. **Serves 12.**

HINT
Preparation may be completed a day ahead. Refrigerate the pears and dressing and assemble just before serving.

PRAWN AND EGG MOUSSE

This super starter, delicately flavoured and light in texture, makes the best of a modest amount of prawns. It is easy and quick to make as there is no need for any accompanying sauce. Serve with melba toast.

400–500 g (14–18 oz) small,
  frozen, uncooked, shelled
  and deveined prawns
25 ml (5 tsp) dry white
  vermouth
10 ml (2 tsp) gelatine
250 ml (8 fl oz) fish (see box,
  page 46) or chicken stock
4 hard-boiled eggs
3–4 spring onions, chopped
125 ml (4 fl oz) mayonnaise
15 ml (1 tbsp) Dijon mustard
125 ml (4 fl oz) cultured soured
  cream
2 egg whites, whisked
milled black pepper and/or
  thin lemon wedges

Tip frozen prawns into a saucepan of rapidly boiling, lightly salted water – enough to cover prawns. Return to boil and cook for about 4 minutes. Drain and chop prawns coarsely. Pour vermouth over. Sponge gelatine in stock, dissolve over low heat and add to prawns. Remove yolks from hard-boiled eggs and set aside. Chop whites finely and add to prawns, together with spring onions. Chill until just starting to thicken. Mix mayonnaise with mustard and fold in, then fold in cream and whisked egg whites. Turn the mixture into eight rinsed ramekins and chill until set.

To serve, unmould onto small serving plates. For garnish, either grate reserved egg yolks over tops and then grind over plenty of black pepper, or use black pepper and a lemon wedge alongside. **Serves 8.**

CHILLED MUSHROOMS WITH TWO STUFFINGS

An excellent, do-ahead starter, in which mushrooms are spread with different pâté-type mixtures. Serve one of each kind on individual plates and accompany with fingers of buttered wholemeal bread. Although herb, chicken or nut stuffings are possibly the most commonly used, the following are more unusual. The mushrooms are lightly grilled and then chilled, ready to be filled at the last moment.

20–24 large brown mushrooms, wiped
sunflower oil
milled black pepper

Slice off mushroom stems and scoop out a little of the centre of each cap and discard. Arrange mushrooms on baking tray, rounded sides up, brush with oil, and place well below pre-heated grill. Grill for 2 minutes, turn, brush again with oil and grill for another 2 minutes, until softening but not floppy. Transfer to plate; season with black pepper – do not use salt, as this will draw out juices. Refrigerate. Drain, if necessary, before serving.

To assemble, fill half the mushrooms with pâté (see below) and scatter with sesame seeds; fill other half with the spread (see alongside) and garnish with chives or parsley. Place one mushroom with pâté and one with spread on each plate and serve as suggested.
Serves 10–12.

COURGETTE PÂTÉ
Adding breadcrumbs to the pâté mixture makes it just firm enough for spreading without masking the delicate courgette flavour. The colour is a light, spring green, and the topping of toasted sesame seeds adds eye appeal and a flavoursome crunch.

30 ml (2 tbsp) sunflower oil
8 spring onions, chopped
2 cloves garlic, crushed
500 g (18 oz) courgettes, pared and sliced
2.5 ml (1/2 tsp) each salt and dried dill
20 ml (4 tsp) water
2 hard-boiled eggs, chopped
30 ml (2 tbsp) mayonnaise
5 ml (1 tsp) Dijon mustard
about 60 ml (4 tbsp) fine, fresh white breadcrumbs
toasted sesame seeds for garnish

Heat oil in a small saucepan, add spring onions and garlic and fry lightly. Add courgettes, salt, dill and water, cover and cook over low heat until soft. If necessary add another dash of water to avoid scorching, but bear in mind that all liquid should be absorbed or purée will be too soft. Add chopped egg, mayonnaise and mustard, tip into food processor fitted with grinding blade, and process until smooth. Add breadcrumbs, a spoonful at a time, and blend well. Mixture will be soft, but will firm up when cold. Spoon into container, cover and chill.
Enough to fill 12 mushrooms.

MUSSEL AND CREAM CHEESE SPREAD
250 g (9 oz) cream cheese
small dash of brandy
4 spring onions, finely chopped
2.5 ml (1/2 tsp) Worcestershire sauce
25 ml (5 tsp) thick mayonnaise
225 g (8 oz) canned mussels in brine, drained and rinsed
milled black pepper
pinch each of salt and sugar
chopped chives or parsley for garnish

Using a wooden spoon, cream all ingredients, except chives or parsley, without mashing mussels completely. Spoon into container, cover and chill.
Enough to fill 10–12 mushrooms.

BAKED STUFFED AVOCADOS

Yes, you can. Avocados will only turn bitter if overheated, and what a lyrical change this recipe is from yesterday's first-course avocado with its ubiquitous filling of shrimps and pink dressing. Use medium, rather than large, avocados, as this is a rich starter. Serve with small spoons and pass a basket of melba toast. This recipe may easily be doubled.

sunflower oil and butter
200 g (7 oz) white mushrooms,
 wiped and chopped
100 g (3½ oz) curd cheese
25 ml (5 tsp) chopped chives or
 finely chopped spring onion
 tops
2.5 ml (½ tsp) soy sauce
pinch each of salt and sugar
2 medium, firm and
 unblemished avocados
a little lemon juice
finely grated Parmesan cheese
paprika

Heat just a slick of oil and a dab of butter in a frying pan, add mushrooms and sauté until just softened and lightly browned. Remove and drain on a paper towel, then mix with curd cheese, chives or spring onion tops, soy sauce, salt and sugar.
  Halve and stone avocados, pour a little lemon juice onto a flat plate and moisten cut surfaces by placing avocado halves, face down, in the juice. Fill avocados with mushroom mixture, smoothing over entire surface – not just hollows. Sprinkle with Parmesan and dust with paprika.
  Arrange avocados slightly apart in a baking dish. Add 2 cm (¾ in) cold water to the dish and bake on middle shelf of oven at 180 ˚C (350 ˚F, gas 4) for 18–20 minutes, or until just heated through. Place each half on a warmed serving plate and serve immediately.
Serves 4.

HINT
If you have oval, individual baking dishes, place half a stuffed avocado in each, add 2 cm (¾ in) cold water to each dish, and bake as above. To serve, tip out the water and run a cloth round the edges of the dishes to remove any spatters.

MEDITERRANEAN SALAD WITH ITALIAN BREAD

This recipe for a superb starter takes the popular tomato-mozzarella salad a step further. The circles of herby, grilled aubergines and Herby Italian Flat Bread (see alongside) add substance to the salad, and the result is a fabulous combination of colours and flavours. It makes a great beginning to a meal of pasta, or a light vegetarian meal with the addition of hard-boiled eggs. No need to wait for the summer either, as I have not used fresh basil.

60 ml (4 tbsp) each sunflower and olive oil
45 ml (3 tbsp) water
5 ml (1 tsp) dried oregano
2.5 ml (1/2 tsp) dried basil
575 g (1 1/4 lb) young aubergines, sliced into rings and dégorged (see box, page 82)

lettuce leaves
575–675 g (1 1/4–1 1/2 lb) firm, ripe tomatoes, sliced
250 g (9 oz) mozzarella or low-fat Edam cheese, thinly sliced milled black pepper

DRESSING
45 ml (3 tbsp) lemon juice
100 ml (3 1/2 fl oz) each sunflower and olive oil
large pinch each of salt and sugar
45 ml (3 tbsp) finely chopped parsley
4 slim spring onions plus some green tops, chopped

Make the dressing by whisking all ingredients together with a fork, and then leave to stand for a few minutes.

Mix oils, water and dried herbs, and pour into a large baking tray. Place tray in oven briefly to heat through, then add aubergine slices in a single layer. Place tray well below grill, to ensure that aubergines are cooked through and not scorched, and grill for 10 minutes. Turn slices and grill for another 10 minutes, or until soft and browned. Cool.

To compose salad, line serving plates with lettuce leaves. Arrange a few aubergine and tomato slices separately on each plate. Top tomatoes with cheese. Grind black pepper over cheese, and then drizzle with dressing. Serve with chunks of freshly baked Italian flat bread.
Serves 8.

HERBY ITALIAN FLAT BREAD

Hoping to persuade even very busy cooks to try this bread, I have started it off in a food processor for really quick mixing. However, there is one brief spell of kneading involved, because I really think it is important to develop a relationship with your dough. There are so many gadgets these days to do the mixing that one forgets what ingredients 'feel' like.

5 ml (1 tsp) instant dried yeast
about 18 rosemary needles
1 large clove garlic, peeled
2.5 ml (1/2 tsp) each salt and sugar
a few sprigs parsley
10 ml (2 tsp) butter
250 g (9 oz) white flour
150 ml (1/4 pint) warm water
1.25 ml (1/4 tsp) salt mixed with 5 ml (1 tsp) water, and grated Parmesan cheese for topping

Place all ingredients, except warm water and ingredients for topping, in a food processor fitted with grinding blade and process until herbs are chopped and ingredients are thoroughly combined. Slowly, while processing, add warm water through feed tube – by the time this has been added, dough should be whizzing round central pivot in a ball. Allow to whiz about 30 times, then transfer the ball – which by now should be soft and smooth – to a bowl brushed

with oil. Turn to coat the dough (to prevent a crust from forming), then cover and leave to rise in a warm place for about 1 hour, or until approximately doubled.

Turn out onto a very lightly floured board and knead well for about 5 minutes. Pat into a 20 cm (8 in) circle, making circle as evenly thick as possible. Place in an oiled layer cake tin to fit, then cover loosely and leave to rise until doubled – about 35 minutes.

Brush top with salted water and sprinkle with Parmesan. Bake at 200 °C (400 °F, gas 6) for 10 minutes, then reduce heat to 180 °C (350 °F, gas 4) and bake for a further 15 minutes. Turn out and serve warm, or cool on a rack until needed.
Makes 1 round, flat loaf.

SALAD WITH MUSHROOMS AND CHEESE BALLS

Starter salads have become increasingly popular. The following is a splendid example – and quite different from the usual Greek, Italian or French. No tomatoes or onion rings here. This salad comprises a simple mixture of salad leaves, tossed with marinated mushrooms and topped with creamy Cheese Balls coated with nuts. Served with crisp, sesame-coated grissini, or Herby Italian Flat Bread (see opposite page), it makes a fashionably elegant beginning to a special dinner.

roughly torn iceberg, oak leaf and red lettuce
shredded young spinach leaves
a handful of bean sprouts (optional)
5 ml (1 tsp) dark sesame oil mixed with 125 ml (4 fl oz) French dressing

MARINATED MUSHROOMS
2 pickling onions, sliced
2 sprigs fresh rosemary
60 ml (4 tbsp) sunflower or olive oil, or combine the two
60 ml (4 tbsp) medium-dry white wine
25 ml (5 tsp) lemon juice
1.25 ml (¼ tsp) salt
30 ml (2 tbsp) chopped parsley
1 bay leaf
5 ml (1 tsp) sugar
125 ml (4 fl oz) water
1 large clove garlic, crushed
250 g (9 oz) small button mushrooms, wiped and stems trimmed

To marinate mushrooms, bring all the ingredients, except mushrooms, to the boil in a saucepan and simmer, covered, for 3–4 minutes. Add mushrooms, cover and poach gently for 5 minutes. Spoon mushrooms and liquid into a wide-based glass bowl (so that they can nestle in liquid), cover and chill overnight or for at least 6 hours. Drain.

To serve salad, toss lettuce, spinach and bean sprouts, if using, with dressing and divide between six serving plates. Top with mushrooms and garnish each plate with four cheese balls.
Serves 6.

CHEESE BALLS
250 g (9 oz) cream cheese
60 g (2 oz) blue cheese, grated
1 pickling onion, grated
2.5 ml (½ tsp) Worcestershire sauce
60 ml (4 tbsp) very fine, fresh white breadcrumbs
60 ml (4 tbsp) finely chopped, toasted pecan nuts

Using a wooden spoon, cream together cheeses, onion and Worcestershire sauce. Mix in crumbs – do not use more than specified, as the mixture will firm up slightly in the refrigerator. Cover and chill. Using a teaspoon, shape into 24 balls and roll in nuts to coat.
Makes 24.

TUNA AND CUCUMBER MOUSSE WITH TOMATO COULIS

Here tuna mousse is elevated to an unusually attractive starter, with the pink tuna mousse topped with a light cucumber cream, and accompanied by a basil-tomato purée. Do not be intimidated by the long list of ingredients – they are all basic and low in cost. Altogether a simple but impressive first course, light in texture, delicate in flavour, and a good choice for novice cooks.

TUNA MOUSSE
15 ml (1 tbsp) gelatine
250 ml (8 fl oz) fish (see box, page 46) or chicken stock
375 g (13 oz) canned tuna in brine, drained
4 spring onions, chopped
a few drops of Tabasco sauce
10 ml (2 tsp) lemon juice
25 ml (5 tsp) tomato sauce
10 ml (2 tsp) anchovy paste
2.5 ml (1/2 tsp) sugar
125 ml (4 fl oz) whipping cream, whipped
1 egg white, stiffly whisked

CUCUMBER CREAM
half a large cucumber, pared and coarsely grated
20 ml (4 tsp) gelatine
125 ml (4 fl oz) chicken stock
2 spring onions, chopped
30 ml (2 tbsp) chopped parsley
125 ml (4 fl oz) mayonnaise
250 ml (8 fl oz) thick Bulgarian yoghurt
salt and milled black pepper
5 ml (1 tsp) sugar
5 ml (1 tsp) Dijon mustard

TOMATO AND BASIL COULIS
25 ml (5 tsp) sunflower oil
1 small onion, chopped
500 g (18 oz) ripe tomatoes, skinned, chopped and preferably seeded
2.5 ml (1/2 tsp) salt
pinch of sugar
25 ml (5 tsp) white wine
25 ml (5 tsp) chopped parsley
20 fresh basil leaves
a little cream or soured cream (optional)

Sprinkle gelatine onto stock, sponge briefly, then dissolve over low heat. Pour into a bowl and add all ingredients, except cream and egg white. Tip into blender goblet and blend until smooth. Turn into a mixing bowl and, using a metal spoon, fold in cream and egg white. Pour into 12 small, rinsed ramekins, dividing equally. They should be two-thirds full. Chill until set.

To make cucumber cream, place grated cucumber in colander, sprinkle with salt, weight, and leave for about 20 minutes. Squeeze dry, using paper towels. Sprinkle gelatine onto stock, sponge and dissolve over low heat, then pour into a bowl. Add cucumber and remaining ingredients. Turn into a blender goblet and blend well.

Pour cucumber cream over set tuna layer to fill ramekins. Refrigerate to set.

To make tomato coulis, heat oil and soften onion without browning. Add tomatoes, salt, sugar, wine and parsley, cover and simmer gently for about 15 minutes, stirring occasionally. Cool slightly, add basil and blend in a blender. Pour into a small container and chill. If using cream, add just before serving.

To serve, unmould ramekins onto serving plates. Spoon a ribbon of the tomato coulis along one side, and serve with small forks. Garnish each mousse simply with two basil leaves.
Serves 12.

ORIENTAL SQUID SALAD

This salad is so unusual, and so delicious, that it invariably becomes a talking point round the dinner table. No deep-frying, no sharp dressings, just a marvellous medley of unlikely ingredients combined to make a memorable starter. Make it in the morning and leave to marinate all day in the refrigerator. Serve in scallop shells, on lettuce leaves, with small rice timbales or in halved avocados. It is important to use really small squid.

300 g (11 oz) small squid, rinsed and sliced into thin rings
250 g (9 oz) button mushrooms, wiped and halved (unless very small)
25 ml (5 tsp) lemon juice
3–4 spring onions, chopped
15 ml (1 tbsp) soy sauce
25 ml (5 tsp) medium-dry white wine

15 ml (1 tbsp) toasted sesame seeds
60 ml (4 tbsp) sunflower oil
pinch of sugar
finely chopped parsley and finely grated lemon rind to garnish

Bring a large saucepan of water to the boil (do not add any salt). Add squid and mushrooms. Return to the boil, then boil rapidly, uncovered, for 3 minutes. Drain well and turn into a shallow glass bowl. Add lemon juice, toss to mix, and cool. Mix remaining ingredients, then combine with squid and mushrooms. Cover and refrigerate for about 8 hours, tossing a few times. Check seasoning – it may need salt and pepper, or a few drops of Tabasco sauce if liked.

Serve as suggested and sprinkle with parsley and just a touch of lemon rind.
Serves 4, or 8 if served in avocado halves.

BAKED TOMATOES WITH HERBS AND MOZZARELLA

Simply a hot version of tomato-and-basil salad. Fashionably light, it makes a fine starter to a dinner in Mediterranean mood, or, being an Italian-style medley, it is also a good choice to serve at a pasta party. Serve in individual baking dishes, or in one large dish if serving as an accompaniment. Use top-quality tomatoes, plenty of cheese, a garnish of fresh basil, and pass hot Garlic and Herb Pittas (see Hint, page 11) to mop up the juices.

45 ml (3 tbsp) olive oil
2 large cloves garlic, crushed
2.5 ml (1/2 tsp) each dried oregano and basil
500 g (18 oz) large, firm tomatoes, well washed and dried
salt and milled black pepper
a few pinches of sugar

1 bunch of slim spring onions plus some green tops, chopped
low-fat mozzarella cheese, thinly sliced
chopped basil for garnish

Mix oil, garlic and dried herbs. Slice tomatoes into 5 mm (1/4 in) thick rings. Arrange half tomato slices in four small baking dishes, or one medium, shallow baking dish. Season with salt, pepper and sugar. Sprinkle with half spring onions and spoon half dressing over. Repeat layers. Cover generously with cheese, and bake, uncovered, at 180 °C (350 °F, Gas 4) for 20–25 minutes. Sprinkle with chopped fresh basil.
Serves 4.

HINT
A good investment is a salt mill; fill it with coarse sea salt, and use with great effect in this and many other recipes.

HERBY MUSHROOMS EN CROÛTE

Brown mushrooms, doused in melted herby butter, topped with cheese and baked on rounds of French bread. Assemble the starter in advance, if necessary, but melt and pour the butter mixture over just before baking. Serve with halved, baked tomatoes or lightly dressed salad leaves.

1 loaf French bread
8 fairly large brown
  mushrooms (about 250 g
  (9 oz)), wiped and trimmed
45 g (1½ oz) butter
45 ml (3 tbsp) olive oil
2 cloves garlic, crushed
60 ml (4 tbsp) chopped, fresh
  herbs*
2.5 ml (½ tsp) salt
milled black pepper
10 ml (2 tsp) lemon juice
mozzarella cheese, sliced

Slice bread about 1 cm (½ in) thick. If using a tapered loaf, slice from centre and at an angle to ensure that each slice is large enough to hold a mushroom. Arrange slices in a lightly oiled, shallow baking dish, and top each with a mushroom, hollow side up. Mix butter, oil, garlic, herbs, seasoning and lemon juice in a small saucepan.

To bake, heat butter mixture until just melted. Stir well to mix, then pour over mushrooms, dividing equally. Top with cheese and bake at 180 °C (350 °F, gas 4) for 18–20 minutes, by which time cheese should have melted, mushrooms have softened, and bread have slowly absorbed juices and crisped. Serve immediately.
Serves 4–8.

* A good combination is 8 large basil leaves, 4 sprigs oregano, a few sprigs of parsley and some chives. If including rosemary, use sparingly.

PRAWNS AND LYCHEES IN CURRY-COCONUT CREAM

Prawns, lychees and a rich, golden dressing make a luscious starter when fresh lychees are available. Serve in halved avocados or simply in lettuce-lined cocktail glasses.

500 g (18 oz) fresh lychees,
  peeled and sliced into
  thin strips
400 g (14 oz) small, shelled and
  deveined cooked prawns,
  thawed if frozen
4 slim spring onions, chopped
paprika, garam masala or milled
  black pepper for garnish

DRESSING
250 ml (8 fl oz) milk
45 g (1½ oz) desiccated
  coconut
10 ml (2 tsp) curry powder
2.5 ml (½ tsp) turmeric
125 ml (4 fl oz) mayonnaise

Make dressing first: place milk, coconut, curry powder and turmeric in a small saucepan and bring slowly to the boil, stirring, to release flavours. Simmer for 1–2 minutes, then remove from hob and stir in mayonnaise. Turn into a blender goblet and blend well. Using a wooden spoon, press through a sieve positioned over a small bowl. Press hard until all moisture is extracted, then discard coconut. Refrigerate the dressing until thickened. Check seasoning, adding a squeeze of lemon juice or a pinch of salt, if necessary.

Place lychees in colander to drain off juices, then pat dry. Mix prawns, lychees and spring onions.

Fold dressing into prawn mixture, then cover and chill for a few hours. Serve as suggested, lightly dusted with garnish of your choice.
Serves 8–10.

GREEN BEAN, SESAME AND RED PEPPER SALAD

An appetite-whetting salad in which slender young beans, crunchy leeks and bright peppers, are married with a dressing touched with the subtly smoky flavour of sesame. Almonds add a sybaritic touch, or alternatively, garnish the salad Greek style, with feta cheese and olives. Either way, the Dilly Mustard Bread (see below) makes a super accompaniment.

60 ml (4 tbsp) sunflower oil
10 ml (2 tsp) dark sesame oil
2 slender leeks, very thinly sliced
400 g (14 oz) young, green beans, trimmed and halved
2 cloves garlic, crushed
1 large red pepper, cored, seeded and thinly julienned
1 walnut-sized knob root ginger, peeled and grated
45 ml (3 tbsp) water
dash sweet sherry
15 ml (1 tbsp) soy sauce
30 ml (2 tbsp) toasted sesame seeds
toasted, slivered almonds or crumbled feta cheese and black olives for garnish

Heat oils in a large frying pan. Add leeks, beans, garlic, red pepper and ginger, and stir-fry until vegetables are coated. Reduce heat, add water, and cook, with lid slightly tilted to retain bright colour, until beans are just tender and water has evaporated. Add sherry and cook for a few minutes more. Stir in soy sauce and sesame seeds and tip mixture into a salad bowl. Set aside to cool, or cover and chill for several hours or overnight. Garnish and serve.
Serves 4–5.

DILLY MUSTARD BREAD
60 g (2 oz) soft butter
5 ml (1 tsp) wholegrain mustard
2.5 ml (1/2 tsp) dried dill
8–10 slices French bread

Cream butter with mustard and dill, spread on bread, place on baking tray and heat through at 180 °C (350 °F, gas 4) for 10 minutes. Serve hot.

MARINATED FETA AND TOMATO PLATTER

A totally unsophisticated starter, but one that is appearing at many stylish parties in place of rich mousses or time-consuming terrines. Marinated for two days in a mixture of oil and fresh herbs, then tumbled in a coating of toasted sesame seeds, these chunks of flavoursome feta are arranged on individual plates together with a variety of accompaniments as suggested below, and served with hot pitta breads or crusty rolls. Full of vitality and vitamins, this is quite one of the brightest choices for a ladies' luncheon.

400 g (14 oz) feta cheese, rinsed and cut into 8 equal portions
100 ml (3¹/₂ fl oz) olive oil
100 ml (3¹/₂ fl oz) sunflower oil
3 large cloves garlic, quartered
6 sprigs thyme
6 sprigs oregano
1 small sprig rosemary, snipped in half
4 small sprigs parsley
2 bay leaves
toasted sesame seeds

ACCOMPANIMENTS
cherry tomatoes or thinly sliced medium tomatoes
onions, sliced into rings
red or yellow peppers, sliced into rings, cored, seeded and blanched (see box alongside)
black olives
lettuce
hot pitta breads or crusty rolls and butter
milled black pepper

Arrange feta in a shallow glass dish to fit snugly, with just enough room to tuck in herbs. Pour oils over and add garlic and herbs, arranging them between and around the chunks of cheese. Cover and refrigerate for about 48 hours (don't leave it for longer as the herby flavour becomes too pronounced), turning cheese occasionally. Drain cheese, and roll each piece in sesame seeds just before serving. **Serves 8.**

HINT
Strain the leftover marinade, add lemon juice to taste, and use to dress green salads.

BLANCHING ONIONS AND PEPPERS
Slice onion into thin rings; slice peppers into rings or strips, discarding ribs and seeds. Place in a bowl, add a pinch of sugar, cover with boiling water and stand for a few minutes. Drain before using.

SPINACH SALAD WITH SESAME RICOTTA BALLS

Shredded spinach and raw mushrooms, tossed with a zingy dressing and topped with Ricotta balls rolled in sesame seeds. Visually this is a beautiful salad, with a harmonious blend of flavours and textures. You must use young, bright green spinach leaves; the Ricotta mixture needs to be made at least 6 hours in advance, to firm up before shaping; and the dressing, too, needs time to stand before using. Serve with hot garlic bread.

1 small bunch of young spinach, shredded
125–250 g (4–9 oz) white mushrooms, wiped and sliced
5 ml (1 tsp) sunflower oil

DRESSING
1.25 ml (¹/₄ tsp) salt
5 ml (1 tsp) Dijon mustard

25 ml (5 tsp) Balsamic or good
  red wine vinegar or lemon
  juice
2.5 ml (¹/2 tsp) sugar
125 ml (4 fl oz) sunflower oil,
  or half sunflower and half
  olive oil
1 sprig rosemary, snipped
  in half

RICOTTA BALLS
250 g (9 oz) Ricotta cheese*
2 spring onions, chopped
30 ml (2 tbsp) chopped parsley
2.5 ml (¹/2 tsp) dark sesame oil
5 ml (1 tsp) soy sauce
25 ml (5 tsp) thick mayonnaise
toasted sesame seeds

Make dressing by combining
salt, mustard, vinegar or lemon
juice, and sugar. Using a fork,
whisk in oil. Add rosemary,
then cover and stand for about
4 hours. Remove rosemary.
  Make Ricotta balls by placing
Ricotta, spring onions, parsley,
sesame oil, soy sauce and mayonnaise in a food processor fitted

with grinding blade. Process
until creamy and well mixed.
Spoon into a container and chill
until firm. Shape into 16 balls,
using 2 teaspoons, and roll in
sesame seeds to coat thoroughly.
  Toss spinach and mushrooms
with oil (this helps the dressing
to adhere) and then with just
enough dressing to add a gloss.
Pile onto individual plates, top
with Ricotta balls and serve.
Serves 4.

* If Ricotta is not available, curd
cheese can be substituted.
However, as this cheese is much
softer than Ricotta, you will have
to reduce mayonnaise by half
and add about 75 ml (5 tbsp)
fine white breadcrumbs, or the
mixture will be too soft to shape.

VARIATIONS
To vary the salad ingredients,
use half spinach and half lettuce
leaves. Cubes of avocado may
also be added, as well as a handful of bean sprouts.

ASPARAGUS AU GRATIN

*This is one recipe for which canned
asparagus is better than fresh, as
the liquid is used in the sauce.*

450 g (1 lb) canned asparagus
  tips and cuts
milk
15 ml (1 tbsp) sunflower oil
15 g (¹/2 oz) butter
6 spring onions, chopped
30 ml (2 tbsp) flour
60 g (2 oz) grated Cheddar
10 ml (2 tsp) Dijon mustard
1.25 ml (¹/4 tsp) salt
large pinch of sugar
45 ml (3 tbsp) fine breadcrumbs
2.5 ml (¹/2 tsp) finely grated
  lemon rind
paprika
a few slivers of butter

Drain asparagus very well, reserving liquid. Measure liquid and
add enough milk to make 300 ml
(¹/2 pint). Heat oil and butter, add

spring onions and soften over
low heat without browning.
Sprinkle in flour, stir until
absorbed, then remove from
heat. Slowly stir in liquid, then
return to hob and stir until
thickened. Reduce heat to very
low and simmer for a few minutes. Remove from heat and add
cheese, mustard, salt and sugar,
stirring until cheese has melted.
  Divide asparagus between six
buttered ramekins, and pour
sauce over, dividing equally. Mix
breadcrumbs with lemon rind,
and sprinkle over. Dust with
paprika and top with slivers of
butter. (Set aside at this stage if
preparing in advance.)
  To bake, place ramekins in a
roasting tin (spaced so they do
not touch, or they could crack).
Pour water into tin to reach two-
thirds up sides of ramekins. Bake
at 180 °C (350 °F, gas 4) for
about 35 minutes, until
browned. Serve plain or with
melba toast.
Serves 6.

SALMON POTS WITH AVOCADO DRESSING

This is a really simple starter that is also low in cost, stretching one can of salmon to feed six people. The custards are creamy and light in texture, while their pale pink colour contrasts with the fresh, green dressing. Bake the custards a day in advance and chill overnight. Whip up the dressing shortly before dinner, then assemble the two just before serving. Serve on their own or with melba toast.

CUSTARDS
200 g (7 oz) canned pink
   salmon
450 ml (³/4 pint) milk
5 ml (1 tsp) anchovy paste
3 eggs
25 ml (5 tsp) medium-dry
   sherry
2.5 ml (¹/2 tsp) salt
1.25 ml (¹/4 tsp) paprika

AVOCADO-CUCUMBER DRESSING
1 medium, ripe avocado,
   peeled and cubed
5 ml (1 tsp) lemon juice
5 ml (1 tsp) chopped chives or
   young spring onion tops
a few drops of Tabasco sauce
a few sprigs parsley
1 x 7.5 cm (3 in) piece
   cucumber, pared, seeded
   and diced
large pinch of salt
large pinch of sugar
15 ml (1 tbsp) medium-dry
   sherry
15 ml (1 tbsp) mayonnaise
a little extra mayonnaise or
   single cream, if necessary
milled black pepper for
   garnish

To make custards, drain salmon, discard any bones, skin and dark flesh, and place in a blender with 250 ml (8 fl oz) of the milk and the anchovy paste. Blend very well. Beat together eggs, remaining milk, sherry, salt and paprika, add salmon mixture and

whisk until thoroughly combined. Pour into six buttered ramekins and place slightly apart in a roasting tin with water to reach two-thirds up sides of ramekins. Bake at 160 °C (325 °F, gas 3) for 45 minutes. Cool in the bain marie. Remove ramekins, cover loosely and refrigerate overnight.

Purée ingredients for dressing in a blender, stopping to scrape down sides as necessary. If too thick to form a smooth purée, add extra mayonnaise or cream. Spoon into a glass jar, drop avocado stone into middle, then cover and chill until needed.

To serve, run a knife round sides of each ramekin and unmould onto individual plates. Flank with a ribbon of dressing and dust with black pepper.
Serves 6.

HINT
To test an avocado for ripeness, shake gently, and if the stone rattles slightly, it is ready to eat.

MUSHROOM AND TWO-CHEESE PÂTÉ

Serve as part of a cheese board at the end of a meal instead of dessert.

30 ml (2 tbsp) sunflower oil
20 g (³/4 oz) butter
250 g (9 oz) white mushrooms,
   wiped and finely chopped
4–6 spring onions, chopped
1–2 cloves garlic, crushed
250 g (9 oz) curd or cream
   cheese
45 g (1¹/2 oz) blue cheese,
   crumbled *
15 ml (1 tbsp) sweet sherry
2.5 ml (¹/2 tsp) Worcestershire
   sauce
salt, pepper or sugar (optional)
walnut halves for garnish

Heat oil and butter, add mushrooms, spring onions and garlic, and sauté over low heat until mushrooms are soft and all liquid has evaporated. Using a wooden spoon, cream cheeses

together with sherry and Worcestershire sauce. Add mushroom mixture and combine thoroughly. Check seasoning, adding salt, milled black pepper or sugar, if necessary, then spoon into a bowl, cover and chill for 24 hours.

Spoon mixture, which should be fairly firm, onto a flat plate and, using a knife dipped into water, shape into a log. Garnish and serve.
Serves 4–6.

* This amount of blue cheese should be enough as the flavour tends to intensify with time.

SPINACH ROULADE WITH SALMON

Based on a soufflé mixture baked in a Swiss roll tin, then rolled up with a creamy filling, roulades make impressive starters or lunch dishes. Usually they may be made several hours in advance and served hot or cold. A simple garnish of lettuce, a slice of avocado dusted with black pepper, and a twist of lemon, is appropriate, although some diners might prefer a dollop of soured cream mixed with snipped chives.

ROULADE
250 g (9 oz) frozen spinach, thawed
1.25 ml (¼ tsp) freshly grated nutmeg
pinch of sugar
60 g (2 oz) butter
45 g (1½ oz) plain flour
375 ml (13 fl oz) hot milk
4 eggs, separated
2.5 ml (½ tsp) salt
2.5 ml (½ tsp) baking powder

FILLING
200 g (7 oz) canned pink salmon
3–4 spring onions, chopped
250 g (9 oz) curd cheese
15 ml (1 tbsp) capers, rinsed and chopped
25 ml (5 tsp) mayonnaise
5 ml (1 tsp) anchovy paste
salt and milled black pepper
a selection of garnishes, as suggested above

To make roulade, place spinach in a small saucepan and cook over low heat until all moisture is absorbed – it must be quite dry. Add nutmeg and sugar, and set aside. Make a thick white sauce with butter, flour and milk. Beat egg yolks with salt, stir into spinach and then mix into white sauce. Pour into a large mixing bowl. Whisk egg whites until stiff peaks form. Using a metal spoon, fold egg whites and baking powder into soufflé mixture. Oil a 33 x 20 cm (13 x 8 in) Swiss roll tin and line with waxed paper, leaving an overlap at ends. (Do not use greaseproof paper.) Oil paper as well, sprinkle with flour, and shake off excess. Pour in roulade mixture, spreading evenly. Bake at 160 ˚C (325 ˚F, gas 3) for about 50 minutes, until lightly browned and springy to touch. Invert tin onto a damp tea-towel. Carefully pull off backing paper and, using towel as an aid, roll up – lengthwise for a thin roulade, widthwise for a fat roulade. Leave to cool.

To make filling, drain salmon, discarding any bones, skin and dark flesh. Mix well with remaining ingredients.

To assemble, carefully unroll roulade and spread filling over, then re-roll. Using a sharp knife, cut off the ends, then slice the remainder into thin slices. Use a spatula to position slices on individual serving plates and garnish as suggested.
Serves 8–10.

CHILLED PEAR AND COURGETTE SOUP

Identifying the ingredients in this soup is often a conversation point. The flavour is fresh and elusive, with just a hint of cinnamon and lemon; the colour is, frankly, pale khaki but this in no way detracts from its appeal, especially if served in white bowls or soup cups, with a pretty garnish. Allow time for the flavours to marry by making it at least 6 hours in advance, and serve very cold. This is a good choice for a summer ladies' luncheon.

25 ml (5 tsp) sunflower oil
15 g (½ oz) butter
2 leeks (white parts only), chopped
1 small onion, chopped
250 g (9 oz) courgettes, pared and sliced
450–500 g (16–18 oz) ripe Packham's Triumph or Bon Chrétien pears, peeled and chopped
1 fairly large potato, peeled and diced
2 slim sticks cinnamon
1 bay leaf
750 ml (1¼ pints) chicken stock, preferably homemade
2 fairly large strips lemon rind, pith removed
about 125 ml (4 fl oz) milk, or half milk and half single cream*
cream and paprika, or a sprig of mint for garnish

Heat oil and butter in a large saucepan. Add leeks, onion, and courgettes, cover saucepan and allow to sweat over low heat for about 10 minutes, shaking pan now and then. Do not brown. Add pears, potato, cinnamon, bay leaf, stock and lemon rind. Cover and simmer gently for about 20 minutes, or until vegetables are soft. Remove from hob and leave to cool to lukewarm, then remove cinnamon stick and lemon rind. Purée in a blender until smooth. Stir in milk or milk and cream, using just enough liquid to thin the soup to the desired consistency. Check seasoning, adding a pinch of sugar and a little salt, if necessary. Chill.
   To serve, float each serving with a dab of cream dusted with paprika, or simply with a pretty sprig of mint.
Serves 6–8.

* To reduce fat content, omit cream and enrich soup with fat-free milk powder. This is a good way of adding creaminess to any smooth soup – use about 60 ml (4 tbsp) milk powder to 125 ml (4 fl oz) milk, and stir until smooth before adding.

CREAM OF BROCCOLI AND APPLE SOUP

Gentle in flavour, pastel in colour, this is what you might call a quietly dignified soup. Savour it either hot or cold, on its own, or as a duo, swirled to one side of the plate, with a bright partner, such as Cream of Butternut Squash Soup (see page 32), providing a glowing colour contrast. Cream soups are best garnished very simply with fresh herbs.

25 ml (5 tsp) sunflower oil
15 g (½ oz) butter
1 pickling onion, chopped
3 large leeks, sliced
300 g (11 oz) broccoli (tough stalks removed), chopped
2 Golden Delicious apples (about 200 g (7 oz)), peeled and cubed
1 litre (1¾ pints) chicken stock

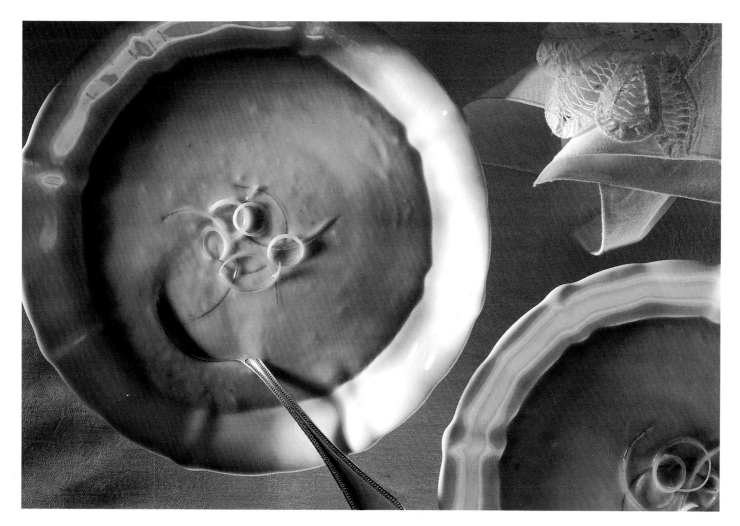

a few sprigs of parsley
2 bay leaves
1.25 ml (¹/₄ tsp) freshly grated
  nutmeg, plus a little extra
2.5 ml (¹/₂ tsp) salt
125 ml (4 fl oz) milk
a little single cream

Heat oil and butter in a large
saucepan, add onion and leeks
and sweat over low heat until
just softened, shaking pan occasionally to prevent catching. Add
broccoli and apples, toss to mix,
then add stock, parsley, bay
leaves, nutmeg and salt. Cover
and simmer gently for about 20
minutes. Remove bay leaves and
add milk. Purée in a blender
until smooth. Return soup to
saucepan and reheat gently, stirring in enough cream to achieve
a velvety consistency, and a
touch of nutmeg to highlight
the flavour. Check seasoning.
  If serving cold, refrigerate for
several hours or overnight.
Serves 6.

AVOCADO VICHYSSOISE

*Avocados make a surprise appear-
ance in this variation on the classic
vichyssoise. Serve hot or cold.*

25 ml (5 tsp) sunflower oil
nut of butter
3 large leeks, sliced
1 small onion, chopped
2 medium potatoes (about
  250g (9 oz)), peeled and
  cubed
1 litre (1³/₄ pints) chicken
  stock
2 bay leaves
1.25 ml (¹/₄ tsp) freshly grated
  nutmeg
2.5 ml (¹/₂ tsp) salt
2 large, ripe and unblemished
  avocados (about 350 g (12 oz)
  each), peeled and cubed
15 ml (1 tbsp) lemon juice
500 ml (17 fl oz) milk
8 thin slivers of avocado and
  milled black pepper, or iced
  vegetables for garnish

Heat oil and butter in a large
saucepan, add leeks and onion,
and soften over low heat, shaking saucepan occasionally to prevent catching. Do not brown.
Add potatoes and toss to mix,
then add stock, bay leaves, nutmeg and salt. Cover and simmer
until vegetables are cooked,
about 20 minutes. Cool to lukewarm. Remove bay leaves. Add
avocados, lemon juice and milk,
then purée in batches in a
blender, until smooth. Check
the seasoning.
  If serving hot, reheat soup
gently in the top of a double
boiler until it is piping hot, but
not boiling. If serving cold, pour
into a container, add avocado
stones, cover and chill for several
hours, or for a full day if more
convenient – colour will hold.
  Serve soup in individual bowls,
and garnish with avocado slivers
and pepper, or with iced
vegetables.
Serves 8.

**ICED VEGETABLE
GARNISH**
*This is a fine, fresh garnish for
cream soups and is made as
follows: slice a leek very thinly,
separate the rings, and drop into
iced water. For added colour,
treat carrots, sliced matchstick-
thin, in the same way. Keep in
refrigerator, and drain well before
sprinkling over soup. This garnish
makes a healthy change from
cream or croûtons.*

CHILLED CUCUMBER, PEAR AND CHEESE SOUP

This soup will probably appeal more to ladies. Generally, men prefer hot and hearty soups, but this one could prove me wrong.

25 ml (5 tsp) sunflower oil
nut of butter
1 cucumber (about 575 g (1¼ lb)), pared and cubed
1 large onion, chopped
5 ml (1 tsp) dried dill
2.5 ml (½ tsp) finely grated lemon rind
750 ml (1¼ pints) chicken stock
2.5 ml (½ tsp) salt
750 g (1¾ lb) ripe, unblemished Bon Chrétien pears, peeled and cubed
125 g (4 oz) cream cheese
very thinly sliced cucumber and milled black pepper to garnish

Heat oil and butter in a large saucepan, add cucumber, onion, dill and lemon rind, and toss over low heat for about 5 minutes. Add stock and salt, and simmer, covered, for 10 minutes. Add pears and simmer for 10 minutes. Remove from heat and leave until no longer steaming. Stir in cream cheese. (If soup is too hot, the cheese might curdle, but it is of no consequence.) Purée in a blender, in batches, until absolutely smooth. Turn into a container and chill, covered, for at least 8 hours. Check seasoning. Spoon into chilled bowls and float with sliced cucumber dusted with pepper. Serves 6.

HINT
When a recipe requires dried dill, use dill tips, not seeds, unless the latter is specified.

CHILLED SWEET-MELON SOUP

The inclusion of this surprising and most delectable soup is due to a food columnist who so much enjoyed it that he specially requested the recipe. It is a good choice to serve to guests with enquiring tastebuds, as the ingredients are elusive, and it makes a super light starter when sweet, amber-fleshed melons are at their peak.

25 ml (5 tsp) sunflower oil
nut of butter
1 medium onion, chopped
2 leeks (white parts only), sliced
5 ml (1 tsp) curry powder
2.5 ml (½ tsp) turmeric
2.5 ml (½ tsp) ground ginger
1 stick cinnamon
2 star anise (optional) *
1 small, ripe sweetmelon, peeled and cubed (about 500 g (18 oz))
500 ml (17 fl oz) chicken stock
250 ml (8 fl oz) milk
a few drops of lemon juice (optional)
double cream and ground cinnamon to garnish

Heat oil and butter in a large saucepan, add onion and leeks, and allow to soften without browning. Add spices and stir for 1 minute over low heat. Add melon cubes, tossing to mix. Add stock. Cover and simmer over very low heat for 15 minutes, until cubes are very soft. Cool for 15 minutes; remove cinnamon stick and star anise, if used. Add milk, then purée in a blender until smooth. Check seasoning, adding, if desired, a few drops of lemon juice to sharpen the flavour. Refrigerate.

Serve in chilled bowls, with a swirl of double cream and a dusting of ground cinnamon, or simply floated with a borage flower, or a sprig of mint. Serves 6.

* The addition of star anise is optional, because I usually try to use ingredients that most cooks have on hand. However, star anise is useful to have for flavouring many Oriental dishes, and is available from speciality shops or the spice counters of larger supermarkets.

☆ Although bread, rolls or toast team up well with hot soup, chilled soups are usually so delicately flavoured that they should be served on their own.

SQUID CHOWDER

A true chowder is an expensive soup, chunky with vegetables and a variety of seafood, with salt pork or bacon added for extra flavour. The following is a much simpler version, more like an Italian soup, with tomatoes and red wine, annelini and a touch of basil doing magic things to a modest amount of squid. Perfect on a chilly night, it makes a meal in itself if served with hot herb bread or rolls. Follow with a salad and a platter of cheese. There is no substitute for the homemade fish stock, and if you cannot get annelini, those minuscule pasta rings, substitute any other tiny noodle to thicken the chowder.

25 ml (5 tsp) olive oil
15 g (½ oz) butter
1 medium onion, chopped
2 leeks, sliced
2 cloves garlic, crushed

300–400 g (11–14 oz) squid rings, halved if large
2 medium potatoes (about 300 g (11 oz)), peeled and diced
400 g (14 oz) canned tomatoes, chopped, plus the juice
10 ml (2 tsp) tomato purée
2 bouquets garnis*
750 ml (1¼ pints) fish stock (see box, page 46)
60 ml (2 fl oz) red wine
60 ml (4 tbsp) chopped parsley
5 ml (1 tsp) sugar
2.5 ml (½ tsp) salt
1.25 ml (¼ tsp) paprika
30 g (1 oz) annelini
a few fresh basil leaves, chopped
grated Parmesan cheese (optional)

In a large, heavy-based saucepan heat oil and butter and soften onion, leeks and garlic. Add squid and toss over medium heat until it stiffens and turns white. Add potatoes and toss to mix, then add remaining ingredients, except pasta, basil and Parmesan.

Bring to the boil, then cover and simmer over very low heat – the soup should barely bubble – for about 1 hour, stirring occasionally to mash tomatoes. Add annelini and simmer for 15 minutes. Remove bouquets garnis and stir in basil (if you don't have fresh basil, omit it, as dried basil won't do).

Ladle into deep, warmed soup bowls, adding a sprinkling of grated Parmesan to each serving, if desired.
Serves 4–5.

* These can be bought, ready tied up in little muslin bags, and are most convenient to use.

A DUET OF PEPPER SOUPS

Serving two (or even three) soups in the same bowl adds up to a starter with real style, and experimenting with different flavours and colours can be fun. The trick is to make the soups thick enough not to melt into each other, but to stay separate, one on each side of the bowl. Almost all cream soups are suitable, and while the colours should afford a bright contrast, neither should be too bold in flavour.

Red and yellow peppers make a striking duo. The basic ingredients and preparation are very similar, and both benefit greatly by using homemade chicken stock rather than a cube. This duet of soups may be served hot or cold.

YELLOW PEPPER SOUP

A delicately spiced soup, the colour of farm butter. Use firm, shiny yellow peppers without wrinkles or soft spots.

350 g (12 oz) yellow peppers
25 ml (5 tsp) sunflower oil
15 g (½ oz) butter
1 medium onion, chopped
2 large leeks, sliced
2.5 ml (½ tsp) each turmeric, ground cumin* and coriander
1 stick cinnamon
1 large potato, peeled and cubed
750 ml (1¼ pints) chicken stock
2.5 ml (½ tsp) each salt and sugar
about 125 ml (4 fl oz) milk

Place peppers in a bowl, cover with boiling water, place a weight on top to prevent them from floating to the surface, and leave for 5 minutes. Drain, slice off tops, discard core and seeds, and chop flesh roughly. In a saucepan, heat oil and butter, add onion, leeks and peppers, and soften without browning. Add spices and sizzle briefly. Add potato and toss to mix. Stir in stock, salt and sugar, cover and simmer for about 20 minutes, or until vegetables are soft. Cool briefly, remove cinnamon stick, and purée mixture in a blender, in batches, until smooth. (A blender is better here than a food processor, as it gives a really smooth result.)

Return to saucepan and reheat gently, stirring in just enough milk to achieve a medium-thick consistency. Chill overnight or reheat before serving.

* For a stronger, more exotic flavour, cumin seeds may be used instead of ground cumin.

RED PEPPER SOUP
Beautifully bright and piquant.

300 g (11 oz) red peppers
25 ml (5 tsp) sunflower oil
15 g (½ oz) butter
1 medium onion, chopped
2 large leeks, sliced
1 large carrot, chopped
2 cloves garlic, crushed
5 ml (1 tsp) paprika
1 large potato, peeled and cubed
750 ml (1¼ pints) chicken stock
2.5 ml (½ tsp) salt
5 ml (1 tsp) sugar
about 125 ml (4 fl oz) milk

Prepare peppers as in previous recipe. Heat oil and butter, add peppers, onion, leeks, carrot and garlic, and allow to soften without browning. Add paprika and potato and toss to mix. Add stock, salt and sugar and simmer, covered, until vegetables are soft. Cool briefly and then purée until smooth. Return to saucepan, and reheat gently, adding enough milk to thin slightly. If serving cold, chill overnight.

To assemble the two soups, ladle a large spoon of each into opposite sides of each bowl. Drop a dollop of cream into the centre and swirl cream into a cobweb, or in circles.
Serves about 10.

LIGHTLY CURRIED PUMPKIN AND APPLE SOUP

Despite the unsophisticated ingredients, this is surely one of the nicest of cream soups. The colour alone will warm the cockles on a cold night, and the subtle mixture of flavours will intrigue. Furthermore, it is downright cheap, may be prepared in advance, and is just as good served cold. Use a bright orange pumpkin with firm flesh.

25 ml (5 tsp) sunflower oil
15 g (½ oz) butter
1 large onion, chopped
500 g (18 oz) peeled pumpkin, cubed (peeled weight)
1 medium potato, peeled and cubed
2 medium Golden Delicious apples (about 200 g (7 oz)), peeled and cubed
2.5 ml (½ tsp) turmeric
5 ml (1 tsp) curry powder
2.5 ml (½ tsp) ground cinnamon
2.5 ml (½ tsp) ground ginger
750 ml (1¼ pints) chicken stock
2.5 ml (½ tsp) salt
1 bay leaf
small pinch of sugar
about 125 ml (4 fl oz) milk
25 ml (5 tsp) brandy
whipped cream or soured cream, and paprika or chopped chives for garnish

Heat oil and butter in a large saucepan, add onion and sauté until golden. Add the pumpkin, potato, apples and spices, and toss together over low heat for about 2 minutes, until coated and smelling good. Add stock, salt, bay leaf and sugar, bring to the boil, then cover and simmer gently until vegetables are soft – about 25 minutes. Cool to lukewarm, then remove bay leaf. Purée mixture until smooth. (If preparing in advance, set aside at this stage.) Return mixture to saucepan and reheat, adding just enough milk to achieve a medium-thick consistency. Add brandy and heat through without boiling.

Ladle soup into warmed soup bowls; top each serving with a blob of cream dusted with paprika or sprinkled with chives. **Serves 6–8.**

CURRIED CREAM OF CAULIFLOWER SOUP

A richly golden, warming start to a meal, this soup contains basic ingredients gently married with Eastern spices. A contrasting garnish of cream dusted with garam masala adds the perfect finishing little bite.

25 ml (5 tsp) sunflower oil
30 g (1 oz) butter
4 leeks (white parts only), sliced
1 small onion, chopped
10 ml (2 tsp) curry powder
5 ml (1 tsp) ground coriander
2.5 ml ($\frac{1}{2}$ tsp) turmeric
2 sticks cinnamon
500 g (18 oz) cauliflower florets
2 medium potatoes, peeled and cubed
1.5 litres (2$\frac{3}{4}$ pints) chicken stock
2 bay leaves
pinch of salt
large pinch of sugar
250 ml (8 fl oz) milk
whipped cream and garam masala for garnish

Heat butter and oil in a large saucepan, add leeks and onion and allow to soften without browning. Add all spices and toss for 1–2 minutes. Add cauliflower and potatoes, and toss to coat, then add stock, bay leaves, salt and sugar. Bring to the boil, then cover and simmer very gently for about 20 minutes, or until vegetables are soft. Remove from hob, add milk and allow to cool slightly. Remove cinnamon stick and bay leaves, then purée until smooth. Return soup to saucepan and reheat over low heat, stirring. Check seasoning.

Ladle soup into warmed soup bowls. Top each serving with a dab of cream and dust lightly with garam masala.
Serves 8.

CREAM OF BUTTERNUT SQUASH SOUP

Velvety and beautifully bright.

25 ml (5 tsp) sunflower oil
15 g ($\frac{1}{2}$ oz) butter
1 onion, chopped
3–4 leeks (white parts only), sliced
2 sticks celery, sliced
500 g (18 oz) peeled butternut squash, cubed (peeled weight)
2 medium potatoes, peeled and cubed
1 litre (1$\frac{3}{4}$ pints) lightly seasoned chicken stock
2.5 ml ($\frac{1}{2}$ tsp) each salt, turmeric and ground ginger
5 ml (1 tsp) sugar
1 fat stick cinnamon
1 bay leaf
250–300 ml (8–10 fl oz) milk
25 ml (5 tsp) sweet sherry
whipped cream and paprika or ground cinnamon for garnish

Heat oil and butter in a large saucepan. Add onion, leeks, celery, butternut squash and potatoes. Cover and sweat over very low heat for about 10 minutes, shaking pan occasionally to prevent catching. Add remaining ingredients, except milk and sherry, bring to the boil, then cover and simmer gently until vegetables are soft. Remove cinnamon stick and bay leaf and cool slightly. Purée the mixture in a blender, in batches, until smooth. Stir in milk and reheat, preferably in the top of a double boiler, then stir in sherry.

To serve, ladle soup into warmed soup bowls. Drop a teaspoon of cream onto each serving and dust with a whiff of paprika or cinnamon.
Serves 6–8.

CHUNKY MUSHROOM, LEEK AND PORT SOUP

Although this soup is made using fresh ingredients, it can be classed as instant as it is so quick to make – yet it is good enough for a dinner party, with a tipple of port adding a special bouquet to the flavour.

25 ml (5 tsp) sunflower oil
15 g (½ oz) butter
1 pickling onion, finely chopped
2 large leeks, thinly sliced
1 clove garlic, crushed
250 g (9 oz) brown mushrooms, wiped and roughly chopped
30 ml (2 tbsp) plain flour
600 ml (1 pint) chicken stock
250 ml (8 fl oz) milk, preferably heated
a pinch of freshly grated nutmeg
15 ml (1 tbsp) soy sauce

salt and milled black pepper
25 ml (5 tsp) port
1 egg yolk*
snipped chives for garnish

Heat oil and butter in a large saucepan, add onion, leeks and garlic and sauté gently. Add mushrooms, and toss until softened. Sprinkle in flour, and when absorbed add stock and milk and stir until thickened. Add nutmeg, soy sauce and seasoning, and simmer, half-covered, over low heat for about 5 minutes. (Do not cover saucepan completely, or soup will boil over.) Whisk together port and egg yolk and add to soup. Stir until very hot, but do not boil.

Ladle into warmed bowls, garnish and serve.
Serves 4.

* The inclusion of flour for thickening makes the addition of the egg yolk optional, for those who prefer a less rich soup.

BEAN, PASTA AND VEGETABLE SOUP

A chunky, substantial meal-in-a-soup, using a can of beans instead of soaking and cooking haricots. A teaspoon of pesto swirled into each serving adds a zip to the flavour, but if you don't have pesto, simply provide freshly grated Parmesan or Pecorino cheese for sprinkling, along with hot rolls, or Herby Italian Flat Bread (see page 16).

30 ml (2 tbsp) olive or sunflower oil
2 onions, chopped
2 cloves garlic, crushed
3–4 carrots, diced
3 sticks celery plus some leaves, sliced
2 litres (3½ pints) chicken or vegetable stock, or a few teaspoons Marmite dissolved in water
125 ml (4 fl oz) tomato passata
100 ml (7 tbsp) chopped parsley

5 ml (1 tsp) salt
2.5 ml (½ tsp) sugar
425 g (15 oz) canned baked beans in tomato sauce
125 g (4 oz) elbow macaroni
90 g (3 oz) finely shredded spinach leaves
2.5 ml (½ tsp) dried oregano
100 ml (3½ fl oz) red wine (optional)

Heat oil in a large saucepan, add onions and garlic and soften without browning. Add carrots and celery and stir-fry briefly. Add stock, tomato passata, parsley, salt and sugar. Cover and simmer for about 25 minutes, until vegetables are cooked. Add remaining ingredients, except wine, return to the boil, then cover and simmer over low heat for 30 minutes, stirring occasionally. Add wine, if using, just before serving.

Serve ladled into warmed soup bowls and garnish each serving as suggested.
Serves 8.

QUICK FISHY SOUPS
The following soups do not aspire to any fancy culinary heights, and you will never meet them in a restaurant. But I include them because they are so jolly useful and quick to make, using unashamedly basic ingredients. One of them even includes fishpaste. Gourmets may simply turn the page.

SPEEDY SALMON SOUP

This very simple soup is pastel pink in colour.

30 ml (2 tbsp) sunflower oil
15 g (½ oz) butter
1 medium onion, chopped
2 medium potatoes (about
    300 g (11 oz)), peeled
    and cubed
5 ml (1 tsp) paprika
750 ml (1¼ pints) lightly
    seasoned chicken stock
425 g (15 oz) canned pink
    salmon, drained
20 ml (4 tsp) anchovy paste
5 ml (1 tsp) Worcestershire
    sauce
150 ml (¼ pint) milk
15 ml (1 tbsp) medium-dry
    sherry
whipped cream and snipped
    chives for garnish

Heat oil and butter in a
saucepan, add onion, and soften
over low heat. Add potatoes and
paprika, and toss for a few
seconds. Add stock, then cover
and simmer gently for about
20 minutes, or until potatoes
are cooked. Pick over salmon,
discarding any skin, bones or
dark flesh, and add, together
with anchovy paste and the
Worcestershire sauce. Heat
through, uncovered, for about
5 minutes, stirring to break up
salmon and melt anchovy paste.
Remove from hob and add milk.
Purée the mixture in a blender
until smooth. (If preparing in
advance, set aside at this stage.)
Add sherry and reheat gently.
Check the seasoning – it may
need salt.
   To offset the pastel pink
colour, swirl a teaspoon of
whipped cream into each serving
and scatter with chives.
Serves 6.

LIGHTLY CURRIED CREAMY MUSSEL SOUP

Although there is nothing to equal the flavour of fresh mussels, they are not always available and that is where this recipe, using canned mussels and the minimum of other ingredients, will prove a real boon. It is a delicious soup – butter-coloured and silky smooth, with a faint lemony tang. It is essential to use homemade fish stock.

900 g (2 lb) canned mussels in shells in brine (about 30 mussels)
25 ml (5 tsp) sunflower oil
a small nut of butter
2 medium onions or 1 small onion and 2 leeks, chopped
5 ml (1 tsp) curry powder
1 clove garlic, crushed
2.5 ml (½ tsp) turmeric, or a few threads saffron soaked in a little hot water
3 medium potatoes (about 400 g (14 oz)), peeled and cubed
750 ml (1¼ pints) fish stock (see box, page 46)
finely grated rind of 1 small lemon
125 ml (4 fl oz) single cream

Drain mussels and rinse very well, discarding any that are closed, then drain again by standing upside down on a plate.
Heat oil and butter, add onions or onion and leeks, curry powder, garlic and turmeric, if using, and sweat over low heat without browning. Add potatoes and toss to mix, then add stock, saffron, if using, and half lemon rind. Cover and simmer gently for about 20 minutes, until potatoes are soft. Cool slightly, then purée until smooth. Return mixture to saucepan and check seasoning – it will probably need a little salt, sugar and enough of the remaining lemon rind to enhance the flavour.

Stir cream and drained mussels into puréed mixture, and reheat, stirring, without boiling.
Ladle into warmed soup bowls and serve with crusty bread.
Serves 4–6.

QUICK CLAM OR OYSTER SOUP

Although this soup requires a good fish stock, the seafood conveniently comes from a can. It should be served freshly made.

15 ml (1 tbsp) sunflower oil
15 g (½ oz) butter
1 medium onion, chopped
2 large leeks (white parts only), chopped
400 g (14 oz) potatoes, peeled and cubed
750 ml (1¼ pints) fish stock (see box, page 46)
2 bay leaves
2.5 ml (½ tsp) salt
300 g (11 oz) canned baby clams in brine or 225 g (8 oz) canned oysters in water, drained
a little milk
15 ml (1 tbsp) medium-dry sherry
fried croûtons, paprika or milled black pepper to garnish

Heat oil and butter in a large saucepan, add onion and leeks and soften without browning. Add potatoes; toss to mix. Add stock, bay leaves and salt; bring to the boil. Cover and simmer until potatoes are soft. Remove bay leaves and add clams or oysters. Purée, then return to saucepan and thin with a little milk. Check seasoning. Add sherry and reheat over low heat, stirring; do not boil. Serve at once, ladled into small, warmed soup bowls. Float croûtons on each serving or dust with paprika or pepper.
Serves 5–6.

FISH WITH A CREAMY SHRIMP SAUCE

Presenting this kind of dish in classic style could involve the cook in a welter of last-minute preparation – poaching the fish, straining the stock, reducing the sauce – a lot of hovering over the cooker, in fact. The following method, however, eliminates much of the fuss, as it uses pre-prepared fish stock. The sauce can therefore be made while the fish is baking, and the assembled dish popped back in the oven for a quick heat-through. A most useful recipe, and certainly good enough for entertaining.

4 large, firm fish fillets,
  skinned (about 675 g (1½
  lb)) (cod is a good choice)
a little salt
lemon juice
30 ml (2 tbsp) sunflower oil
30 g (1 oz) butter
60 ml (4 tbsp) flour
500 ml (17 fl oz) hot fish stock
  (see box, page 46)
60 ml (4 tbsp) single cream
200 g (7 oz) canned shrimps in
  brine, drained and rinsed
15 ml (1 tbsp) medium-dry
  sherry
10 ml (2 tsp) capers, rinsed
  and chopped

Arrange fillets in a large, buttered baking dish, without overlapping. Sprinkle with salt and lemon juice, and bake at 160 °C (325 °F, gas 3) for 25–30 minutes, until just cooked without any juices starting to run. (Exact baking time will depend on thickness of fillets.)

Meanwhile, make sauce. Heat oil and butter, add flour and stir over low heat until absorbed. Slowly stir in stock and, when sauce is smooth, allow to simmer very gently for about 10 minutes until consistency of fairly thick cream. Add remaining ingredients and check seasoning.

Pour sauce over fish, return to oven briefly to heat through, and serve with tiny jacket potatoes and vegetables.
Serves 4.

FISH PUFF

So many recipes call for fresh, firm fish that it is quite a relief to find one that may be baked straight from the freezer. Hake or bream is the best fish to use here. Because the topping is feather-light and non-cloying, it will not complement a fish that comes in thick, firm fillets, making this recipe good news for any cook in search of family fare with a little panache. As this is a simple dish, serve it simply, with creamy mashed potatoes and vegetables.

5–6 fairly thin fish fillets,
  skinned (about 800 – 900 g
  (1¾–2 lb))
seasoned flour for coating
finely grated lemon rind

TOPPING
60 ml (4 tbsp) mayonnaise
60 ml (4 tbsp) cultured soured
  cream
4 spring onions, chopped
5 ml (1 tsp) pale Dijon mustard
  or tarragon mustard
2.5 ml (½ tsp) crushed dried
  tarragon or 15 ml (1 tbsp)
  chopped fresh dill
2 egg whites, stiffly whisked
a pinch of paprika

Make a few diagonal slashes on skinned side of fish to prevent curling, and dust both sides with seasoned flour. Arrange in a single layer in a large, well-buttered baking dish. Sprinkle a little lemon rind on each piece and bake at 180 °C (350 °F, gas 4) for 10 minutes, allowing an extra 5 minutes if the fish is baked from frozen.

Meanwhile, make topping by combining mayonnaise, soured cream, onions, mustard and chosen herb. Fold in egg whites. Remove fish from oven, spoon

topping over to cover complete-ly, and dust with paprika.

Return dish to oven for 15–20 minutes until topping is puffy and fish flakes easily when tested with a fork. Serve immediately as suggested.
Serves 5–6.

WHOLE BAKED FISH WITH YOGHURT AÏOLI

Try this once, and you're bound to be hooked. Surrounded with vegetables, dotted with fresh herbs, doused with wine and oil and then baked, this recipe is a top favourite, using a firm, fresh fish such as bass. Serve hot, accompanied by tiny potatoes boiled in their jackets. Alternatively, serve the fish at room temperature with the Yoghurt Aïoli (see alongside) – it is fabulous either way.

1.25 kg (2³⁄₄ lb) whole fresh bass (including the head), cleaned, scaled and with fins and backbone removed
salt and milled black pepper
6 sprigs thyme
4 sprigs oregano
1 small lemon, thinly sliced
2–3 tomatoes, skinned and chopped
8 large pickling onions, quartered
2 cloves garlic, crushed
250 g (9 oz) courgettes, pared and sliced into rings
250 g (9 oz) white mushrooms, wiped and quartered
a handful of chopped parsley
3–4 bay leaves
250 ml (8 fl oz) water
125 ml (4 fl oz) medium-dry white wine
100 ml (3¹⁄₂ fl oz) sunflower oil
10–15 ml (2–3 tsp) cornflour (optional)

Season cavity of fish and tuck in half herbs and half lemon slices, then place flat in a very large baking dish – if necessary, cut off tail. Mix vegetables and parsley, spoon round fish; season. Tuck bay leaves into vegetables. Mix water, wine and oil; drizzle over fish and vegetables. Place rest of herbs and lemon slices on top.

Cover loosely with oiled greaseproof (not waxed) paper and bake at 180 °C (350 °F, gas 4) for 50 minutes, until vegetables have softened and fish flakes easily when tested with a fork. Remove herbs and lemon slices. Using two spatulas, lift fish onto a large, heated serving platter. Using a slotted spoon, remove vegetables; arrange round fish or on a separate platter.

Tip the lovely juices into a small saucepan and thicken with cornflour slaked with a little water. Boil up and serve separately. If serving at room temperature, simply stand for about 30 minutes until juices lose their heat, then serve.
Serves 4.

YOGHURT AÏOLI
The addition of yoghurt lightens this rich mayonnaise and softens the strong flavour of garlic.

3–4 large cloves garlic, crushed
1 extra-large egg
2.5 ml (¹⁄₂ tsp) salt
5 ml (1 tsp) sugar
25 ml (5 tsp) lemon juice
200 ml (7 fl oz) sunflower oil
4 spring onions, finely chopped
125 ml (4 fl oz) thick Bulgarian yoghurt

Place garlic, egg, salt, sugar, lemon juice and 25 ml (5 tsp) of the oil in a blender and blend well. Add the remaining oil very slowly, while blending. Mixture will emulsify to a thick mayon-naise. Spoon into a small glass bowl, fold in spring onions and yoghurt, cover and chill for sev-eral hours before serving.
Makes about 375 ml (13 fl oz).

BAKED FISH À LA CRÈME

No cookbook of the 1990s would be complete without at least one recipe using a cherished ingredient in French cuisine – crème fraîche. Made by treating cream with a certain culture which gives it a slightly sour tang, it is a product peculiar to France, although cooks in other countries have been quick to come up with a good substitute. This mock crème fraîche is often welcomed as a light alternative to double cream, but sadly this is not accurate. Made by souring and thickening sweet cream with a little buttermilk, it is every bit as rich and fattening. Before splashing out on the following recipe, refer to the box on this page for more information on crème fraîche.

575 g (1¼ lb) long, fairly thin, skinned fillets (or other firm, non-oily fish)*
seasoned flour for coating

1 bunch of slim spring onions, chopped
200–250 ml (7–8 fl oz) crème fraîche
7.5 ml (1½ tsp) pale, mild Dijon mustard
5 ml (1 tsp) pale, thin honey
10 ml (2 tsp) brandy
pinch of sugar
paprika

Cut fish into 4 pieces, pat dry on paper towels and roll in seasoned flour. Arrange in a buttered dish to fit snugly. Sprinkle each fillet with spring onions. Whip crème fraîche with mustard, honey, brandy and sugar. Spoon over fish and dust with paprika.
    Bake at 200 °C (400 °F, gas 6) for about 20 minutes, or until fish is cooked.
Serves 4.

* It is important to use fish that is not too thick to avoid prolonged baking and possible scorching of the crème fraîche round the edges.

CRÈME FRAÎCHE
Pour 250 ml (8 fl oz) cream into a sterilized glass jar. Add 30 ml (2 tbsp) buttermilk, whisk lightly, using a fork, then close jar and leave in a warm place until thickened. This can take 24 hours or longer in cold weather. Chill for at least a day before using – it will thicken further in the refrigerator and the tang will become more pronounced.
    Crème fraîche keeps well, holds its shape, and can be lightened to serve with sweet desserts by whipping 250 ml (8 fl oz) with 75 ml (5 tbsp) iced water.

FISH IN A LIGHT CURRY SAUCE

This is a fine example of how to dress up economical hake for guests. The fact that hake is not a firm fish is an advantage here, as this allows it to absorb the flavours in the subtly spiced sauce, and the result is an unusual treat. Serve with rice, chutney and a tomato salad.

30 ml (2 tbsp) sunflower oil
1 medium onion, chopped
1 stick cinnamon
2.5 ml (½ tsp) turmeric
10 ml (2 tsp) curry powder
5 ml (1 tsp) ground fennel
5 ml (1 tsp) ground coriander
2.5 ml (½ tsp) ground cumin
about 675 g (1½ lb) skinned, fresh hake fillets, cut into 4 pieces
salt and white pepper
250 ml (8 fl oz) milk
45 g (1½ oz) desiccated coconut
garam masala

Heat oil in a large frying pan. Add onion and spices and toss over very low heat for 1–2 minutes – do not allow onion to brown. Place hake fillets on top of onions, without overlapping. If mixture seems dry, add a dash of water. Cook, still over very low heat, until fillets are bright yellow on the undersides (lift and peek). Turn carefully, using a spatula, and season lightly. Mix milk with coconut and add to pan. Cover and cook gently – liquid should just bubble – for about 10 minutes, or until fish is cooked.

Carefully transfer fish to a serving platter and keep warm in the oven at 160 °C (325 °F, gas 3). Cool sauce briefly, then purée in a blender.

Remove fish from oven and press sauce through a sieve directly over fish so that it coats it evenly. Consistency of sauce should be that of slightly thickened cream. (A little juice might have escaped from fish while it

was keeping warm, but this will amalgamate with sauce.) Discard coconut left in the sieve. Sprinkle with a little garam masala, and return dish to the oven for about 10 minutes to heat through before serving. **Serves 4.**

PERNOD FISH FLORENTINE

A bed of spinach and a sauce laced with Pernod transform any fish into something special, and the fact that you can use the humblest of species, such as bream or hake, means it is actually a budget dish — but with an upmarket flavour. Another plus is that you do not need to make a fish bouillon, and also, the dish may be assembled in advance. Served with fluffy, lemon-flavoured rice and stir-fried courgettes, it makes a delicious meal for friends or family.

500 g (18 oz) frozen spinach, thawed
salt and a pinch of freshly grated nutmeg
200 ml (7 fl oz) water
200 ml (7 fl oz) milk
a few black peppercorns
pinch of salt
a few sprigs of parsley
2 bay leaves
750 g (1 ¾ lb) bream or hake fillets, skinned
20 g (¾ oz) butter
20 ml (4 tsp) sunflower oil
60 ml (4 tbsp) flour
100 ml (3 ½ fl oz) cream
20 ml (4 tsp) Pernod
grated cheese of choice, preferably Parmesan

Drain spinach in a colander, pressing out all moisture. Season lightly with salt and nutmeg; spread on base of a buttered baking dish with fairly high sides as the sauce will bubble up. Place water, milk, peppercorns, salt, parsley and bay leaves in a large frying pan. Add fish fillets in a

single layer and slowly bring to the boil. Poach gently until just cooked.

Remove fish with slotted spoon and arrange on top of spinach. Strain poaching liquid — you should have 400 ml (14 fl oz). Heat butter and oil in small saucepan, add flour and stir until straw-coloured. Remove from heat and slowly stir in hot poaching liquid, then return to hob and stir until boiling. Once thickened and smooth, allow to bubble gently for a few minutes. Stir in cream and cook for a few minutes more, then remove from hob and add Pernod. Check seasoning, then pour sauce evenly over fish. (Dish may be prepared in advance to this point — if weather is warm, refrigerate, but return to room temperature before baking.) Sprinkle with cheese and bake at 200 °C (400 °F, gas 6) for 20 minutes. **Serves 4.**

BAKED FISH WITH A LIGHT ORANGE-GINGER SAUCE

Frozen fish does have its limitations, but it certainly is a most useful item. Usually best cooked from frozen, perfect for quickly prepared, budget meals, the following recipe is a fine example. Super with rice tossed with fried mushrooms and grated lemon rind.

200 ml (7 fl oz) fresh orange
  juice
5 ml (1 tsp) finely grated
  lemon rind
half a bunch of spring onions,
  chopped
25 ml (5 tsp) soy sauce
2.5 ml (½ tsp) brown sugar
1 walnut-sized knob root
  ginger, peeled and finely
  chopped
30 ml (2 tbsp) chopped parsley
1.25 ml (¼ tsp) Five-Spice
  Powder (optional)*
25 ml (5 tsp) sunflower oil
15 g (½ oz) butter
675 g (1½ lb) frozen, skinned
  hake or whiting fillets
15 ml (1 tbsp) cornflour
25 ml (5 tsp) medium-dry
  sherry
45 ml (3 tbsp) single cream
toasted sesame seeds for
  garnish

Mix orange juice, lemon rind, spring onions, soy sauce, sugar, ginger, parsley and Five-Spice Powder, if using. Heat oven to 180 °C (350 °F, gas 4). Place oil and butter in a 28 x 23 cm (11 x 9 in) glass or porcelain baking dish; heat in oven. Arrange fillets in a single layer in the hot dish, without overlapping. Pour sauce over fish; bake, uncovered, for 20 minutes. Mix cornflour with sherry and cream, stir into sauce and bake for a further 15–20 minutes, until fish is cooked. Using a slotted spoon, carefully lift fillets onto warmed serving platter, stir the sauce to smooth it, pour over fish and sprinkle with sesame seeds.
Serves 4.

* Chinese Five-Spice Powder is a mixture of several spices, including star anise, cloves, cinnamon and fennel, and is popular in Oriental pork and beef dishes. Use sparingly.

FISH AND SHRIMP CUSTARD WITH TOMATO SALSA

Instead of making fish cakes, present plebeian minced hake in a new guise. This could be called a novelty dish with strong ethnic connections, and one which will surely intrigue guests, who are unlikely to have eaten it before. Baking the mixture in a bain marie and using a generous quantity of custard ensure that the dish is not dry, while the accompanying salsa adds a fresh bite. The given quantities of curry powder and chilli sauce result in a mild rather than hot flavour, and may be increased to taste. Serve with Salsa and Yellow Rice (see box alongside).

1 thin slice crustless bread
375 ml (13 fl oz) milk
25 ml (5 tsp) sunflower oil
20 g (1/2 tsp) butter
1 large onion, finely chopped

2 cloves garlic, crushed
15 ml (1 tbsp) curry powder (or more to taste)
2.5 ml (1/2 tsp) each turmeric and ground cumin
5 ml (1 tsp) each ground fennel and coriander
500 g (18 oz) minced white fish (such as hake)
5 ml (1 tsp) salt
45 ml (3 tbsp) chutney
15 ml (1 tbsp) lemon juice
200 g (7 oz) canned shrimps in brine, drained and rinsed
3 eggs
75 ml (5 tbsp) desiccated coconut
2.5 ml (1/2 tsp) each salt and turmeric
a few bay leaves, or fresh curry leaves, rinsed in salt water and soaked

Soak bread in milk. Heat oil and butter and soften onion and garlic. Add all the spices and toss over low heat until onion is coated. Remove from hob and mix into fish, together with salt,

chutney, lemon juice, shrimps and 1 beaten egg. Do not over-mix. Squeeze milk from bread and add bread to mixture, reserving milk. Working very lightly, spoon mixture levelly into a buttered 23 cm (9 in) square baking dish. Beat remaining eggs with reserved milk, coconut, salt and turmeric, and pour over fish. Insert bay or curry leaves.

Place dish in a large roasting tin, add cold water to tin to reach two-thirds up the sides and bake at 160 °C (325 °F, gas 3) for 1 hour 10 minutes, or until set.
Serves 6.

TOMATO SALSA
250 g (9 oz) ripe but firm tomatoes
4 spring onions, chopped
1 large yellow pepper, cored, seeded and finely diced
2.5 ml (1/2 tsp) sugar
10 ml (2 tsp) chilli sauce (or to taste)
1 small clove garlic, crushed
milled black pepper

Wash and dry tomatoes well, and chop into small pieces. Mix all ingredients – do not add any salt as the juices should not be drawn. Cover and refrigerate for a few hours before serving.

YELLOW RICE
Put 200 g (7 oz) long-grain white rice, 500 ml (17 fl oz) water, 2.5 ml (1/2 tsp) each salt and turmeric, 1–2 sticks cinnamon and 45 g (1 1/2 oz) seedless raisins in a saucepan. Bring to the boil, then reduce heat, cover, and simmer for 20–25 minutes until water is absorbed. Remove cinnamon sticks. If using brown rice, add an extra 45 ml (3 tbsp) water and cook for 50 minutes. To avoid catching, brush base of saucepan with oil before adding ingredients.

BUTTER-BAKED FISH WITH RED PEPPER SAUCE

In this recipe a purée of peppers, delicate in flavour but vivacious in colour, is used to spark up white fish fillets. You can use fresh fish, or frozen hake straight from the freezer. You can serve the fish hot, with a ribbon of the purée along-side, or you can coat the baked fish with the purée, and return it to the oven to heat through. You could even serve it cold, as a flamboyant fish salad. Garnished with fresh green herbs, this dish really is as pretty as a picture.

450–500 g (16–18 oz) fish
  fillets, skinned
60 g (2 oz) butter
1 clove garlic, crushed
15 ml (1 tbsp) finely chopped
  chives
15 ml (1 tbsp) lemon juice
seasoned flour for coating

SAUCE
2 fairly large red peppers
  (about 175 g (6 oz)), seeded,
  cored and roughly chopped
1 small onion, chopped
1 clove garlic, halved
1.25 ml (¹/₄ tsp) each salt and
  paprika
2.5 ml (¹/₂ tsp) sugar
100 ml (3¹/₂ fl oz) chicken or
  vegetable stock (if using a
  cube, use a quarter cube)
about 30 ml (2 tbsp) thick
  mayonnaise

Start by making sauce: place all ingredients, except mayonnaise, in a small saucepan, bring to the boil, then cover and simmer gently for 10–15 minutes, until peppers are soft. Cool slightly, then purée in a blender until smooth. Press through a sieve. Stir in mayonnaise, using just enough to add a creamy richness without diluting flavour of peppers. Set aside.

To prepare fish, make two or three diagonal slashes on the skinned side of each fillet, so that they do not curl up during baking. Melt butter with garlic, chives and lemon juice. Brush mixture on both sides of fillets. Dip into seasoned flour, shaking off excess.

Arrange fillets in a single layer in a lightly oiled baking dish. Cover loosely with oiled grease-proof paper and bake at 200 °C (400 °F, gas 6) – 15–20 minutes for fresh fish, 20–25 minutes for frozen fish. Test with a fork, as baking times will vary depending on thickness of fillets.
Serves 3–4.

FISH SUPRÊME

Suprême is a word with different culinary meanings. It could denote a fillet of chicken, a sauce with eggs and cream, or simply a splendid way of cooking and presenting a dish using fine ingredients. The latter applies to this dish, which is, to my mind, one of the best ways of serving fish – steamed on a bed of simmering vegetables, with a savoury beurre manié to bind the sauce. Light and pure and quick, and a superb way of preparing a succulent fish such as halibut. Careful cooking is very important in this case and I suggest you try it on the family first, so that you can get the timing just right, before treating your guests.

125 ml (4 fl oz) dry vermouth
125 ml (4 fl oz) water
300 g (11 oz) courgettes, pared
  and thinly julienned
1 bunch of spring onions,
  chopped
2 sticks celery plus some
  leaves, finely chopped
2.5 ml (¹/₂ tsp) salt
250 g (9 oz) white mushrooms,
  wiped and thinly sliced
575 g (1¹/₄ lb) filleted and
  skinned halibut loin, cut into
  4 pieces
salt and milled black pepper

BEURRE MANIÉ
30 g (1 oz) butter
20 ml (4 tsp) flour
2.5 ml (¹/₂ tsp) very finely grated lemon rind
15 ml (1 tbsp) chopped fresh dill

Put vermouth, water, courgettes, spring onions, celery and salt in a large frying pan. Bring to the boil, then cover and simmer gently for 8 minutes. Keep heat very low as liquid must not boil away. Add mushrooms, place fish on top, and season lightly. Cover and simmer for about 10 minutes, or until fish flakes easily. Lift fish onto serving dish and keep warm.

Mix ingredients for beurre manié to a smooth paste. Allow vegetable sauce to come off the boil, then add beurre manié in small pats, stirring. Return to the boil to thicken, then spoon the mixture over fish and serve.
Serves 4.

FISH FILLETS IN MUSHROOM SAUCE

This light sauce is delicately flavoured with rosemary and mustard.

30 ml (2 tbsp) sunflower oil
20 g (³/₄ oz) butter
4–6 firm fish fillets, skinned (about 750 g (1³/₄ lb))
salt and milled black pepper
6 spring onions plus some of the tops, chopped
60 ml (4 tbsp) medium-dry sherry
1 small sprig rosemary, needles finely chopped
45 ml (3 tbsp) flour
250 ml (8 fl oz) fish stock (see box, page 46) or light chicken stock
250 ml (8 fl oz) milk
10 ml (2 tsp) Dijon mustard
250 g (9 oz) white mushrooms, wiped and thinly sliced
chopped parsley for garnish

Heat oil and butter on medium heat in a large, heavy-based frying pan, and seal fish quickly on both sides – do not brown or cook through. Using a slotted spoon, remove fish, season and set aside. Reduce heat to low, add onions, sherry and rosemary to pan, and allow to bubble for a few seconds until marvellously aromatic. Sprinkle in flour, then slowly stir in stock, milk and mustard, and simmer until thickened. Add mushrooms and simmer, stirring, until mushrooms have softened. They will release some moisture and thin sauce slightly. Return fish to pan, and cook very gently, half-covered, until just done – this takes a few minutes only. Check seasoning.

Carefully lift fish into serving dish, pour sauce over, garnish and serve.
Serves 4–6.

(see box, page 46)

HERBY CREAM SAUCE
125 ml (4 fl oz) cream
125 ml (4 fl oz) fish (see box, page 46) or chicken stock
30 ml (2 tbsp) each finely chopped parsley and chives
12 large, fresh basil leaves, finely shredded
125 ml (4 fl oz) milk
5 ml (1 tsp) Dijon mustard
large pinch each of salt and sugar
25 ml (5 tsp) cornflour
15 ml (1 tbsp) brandy

To make the sauce, place cream, stock, parsley, chives, basil, milk, mustard, salt and sugar in a small saucepan. (If working ahead, set aside at this stage.) Stir in cornflour mixed with brandy, and heat, stirring, until thickened and just bubbling. Check seasoning, add a nut of butter and pour sauce over cooked fish.
Serves 4.

FISH WITH ANCHOVY MAYONNAISE

This dish is perfect for a cold buffet. The dressing of mayonnaise, lightened with fish stock and firmed up with a little gelatine, is used to coat single-serving fillets. Garnish and surround with Pasta Salad.

1 kg filleted and skinned, firm
  fish (such as Cape salmon)
capers, olives and lemon twists
  for garnish

ANCHOVY MAYONNAISE
1 egg
25 ml fresh lemon juice
225 ml sunflower oil
5 ml sugar
1 ml paprika
1 x 50 g can rolled anchovies
  with capers, soaked in milk
  for 1 hour, then drained
5 ml gelatine
125 ml reserved fish stock

Cut fish into three large pieces and place in a frying pan. Add water to almost cover fish, 50 ml white wine, 2 bay leaves, 1 quartered onion, 5 ml salt, a few peppercorns, 1 halved carrot and a few tufts of parsley. Slowly bring to the boil, reduce heat immediately and poach very gently until just cooked through. Cool in the stock, then remove fish with a slotted spoon. Strain stock.

To make the mayonnaise, place egg, lemon juice, 25 ml of the oil, the sugar and paprika in blender goblet and blend well. Slowly add the remaining oil while blending. When the mixture is thick and smooth, add the anchovies and blend thoroughly. Turn into a bowl. Sponge gelatine in the reserved stock, dissolve over low heat, and slowly stir into mayonnaise. Chill until just starting to thicken.

Divide cold, well-drained fish into neat shapes, scraping away any dark flesh and extracting any errant bones. Arrange on a large, flat serving platter. Carefully spoon over a little of the mayonnaise, repeating several times to coat.
Serves 8.

PASTA SALAD
250 g elbow macaroni
75 ml oil (olive or
  sunflower oil)
30 ml fresh lemon juice
1 large clove garlic, crushed
2 ml salt
50 ml chopped fresh basil
2 medium tomatoes, chopped
100 ml chopped parsley
half a bunch of spring onions
1 x 10 cm piece English
  cucumber, pared, seeded
  and diced

Cook pasta and drain well. Mix oil, lemon juice, garlic and salt and fork into hot pasta. Add remaining ingredients, toss to mix, then cover loosely and stand for 1 hour before serving.
Serves 8.

CRUMBED FISH WITH CHUNKY GUACAMOLE

A super alternative to fried fish, which requires last-minute attention. All the preparation is done in advance, including the guacamole. This is not the regular, hot Mexican dip, but a variation. The chillies, which would be altogether too overpowering for the lemony fish, have been omitted, and fresh basil has been included. Serve fish with potatoes mashed with plenty of hot milk and butter.

50 ml mayonnaise
10 ml fresh lemon juice
10 ml chopped chives
4 firm, succulent fish fillets,
  skinned (500–600 g)
125 ml fine, packaged
  breadcrumbs
2 ml salt
5 ml finely grated lemon rind
sunflower oil for baking

CHUNKY GUACAMOLE
**1 medium to large avocado,
  peeled, diced and tossed in
  10 ml (2 tsp) lemon juice
1 large tomato, skinned,
  seeded and finely chopped
3 spring onions, chopped
pinch each of salt and sugar
milled black pepper
4 large, fresh basil leaves,
  chopped
a few drops of Tabasco sauce**

First make guacamole: place all
ingredients in a small pottery
dish and mix gently, using tip of
a sharp knife so as not to mash.
Push avocado stone into the centre (this will help to preserve
colour), cover and chill for up to
3 hours. Remove stone before
serving.

Mix mayonnaise, lemon juice
and chives on a large plate. Dry
fish well with paper towels and
make a few diagonal slashes on
the skinned side. Coat fish on
both sides with mayonnaise mixture. On a separate plate, mix

breadcrumbs, salt and lemon
rind. Roll fish in crumb mixture,
patting on firmly, then chill for
at least 1 hour to set crumbs.

Cover base of an ovenproof
glass dish – large enough to take
fish without overlapping – with
a thin layer of oil and heat in
oven at 180 °C (350 °F, gas 4).
Turn fillets once in hot oil and
then bake, uncovered, for 20–25
minutes, until just cooked.

Using a spatula, lift fillets onto
a warmed platter. Serve with
chilled sauce.
Serves 4.

ORIENTAL FISH

*The ingredients are pure and simple,
preparation is a pleasure, and the
flavour is aromatically alluring.
Simmered in a sauce with a waft of
lemon, sesame and ginger, these
fish fillets make perfect fare for
entertaining, and the fresh flavour
will delight gourmet guests. Lemon
grass imparts an inimitable touch.
If unavailable in your neighbour-
hood, substitute a little grated
lemon rind.*

**500 g (18 oz) fairly thin,
  skinned fish fillets (such as
  bream)
seasoned flour for coating
45 ml (3 tbsp) sunflower oil
10 ml (2 tsp) dark sesame oil
1 bunch of spring onions,
  chopped
2 cloves garlic, crushed
1 walnut-sized knob root
  ginger, peeled and finely
  chopped
250 g (9 oz) white mushrooms,
  wiped and thinly sliced
125 ml (4 fl oz) medium-dry
  white wine
125 ml (4 fl oz) vegetable or
  fish stock
6 x 10 cm (4 in) pieces lemon
  grass, or a little grated
  lemon rind
25 ml (5 tsp) soy sauce
pinch of sugar
toasted sesame seeds to garnish**

Make a few diagonal slashes on
skinned side of fish to prevent
curling. Dust with seasoned flour
and shake off excess. Heat oils in
a large frying pan, add fish and
quickly seal on both sides. Use a
slotted spoon to remove from
pan, and set aside.

To pan add spring onions, garlic, ginger and mushrooms with
a dash of water if fish has
absorbed all oil. Toss over low
heat until mixture is dry, mushrooms are softening, and ginger
and garlic releasing a wonderful
aroma. Add remaining ingredients, except sesame seeds, stir to
mix and when just bubbling
slide fish back into pan. Simmer,
half-covered, over very low heat
– keep liquid at a gentle bubble –
for about 10 minutes, or until
fish is cooked through and sauce
reduced. Remove lemon grass.

Place fish on warmed serving
platter, pour sauce over, and
sprinkle with sesame seeds.
Serves 4.

PRAWN AND MUSHROOM PILAFF

Pilaffs are perfect for busy cooks and may be as simple or as fancy as you please. The basic mixture is fried onion and rice cooked in a flavoursome stock, to be served as an accompaniment to a meal, but you can add interest with all sorts of additions. The inclusion of vegetables makes it more substantial while the addition of meat, poultry or fish transforms a pilaff into a light main dish. The following delicious version requires a good, home-made fish stock. Serve with a dressed green salad.

400 g (14 oz) cooked, shelled
  and deveined small prawns,
  thawed if frozen
25 ml (5 tsp) sherry
25 ml (5 tsp) sunflower oil
30 g (1 oz) butter
1 onion, chopped

1 red pepper, cored, seeded
  and diced
2 cloves garlic, crushed
250 g (9 oz) white mushrooms,
  wiped and sliced
5 ml (1 tsp) dried tarragon,
  crushed between the fingers
2.5 ml (1/2 tsp) turmeric
200 g (7 oz) long-grain white
  rice
500 ml (17 fl oz) hot fish stock
  (see box alongside)
100 ml (7 tbsp) chopped
  parsley
2.5 ml (1/2 tsp) salt
2.5 ml (1/2 tsp) finely grated
  lemon rind
45 ml (3 tbsp) grated Parmesan

Place prawns in a bowl, add sherry and leave to soak while cooking the rice mixture.
  Heat oil and butter in a large frying pan. Add onion, red pepper and garlic, and allow to soften but not brown. Add mushrooms, toss well, then add tarragon, turmeric and rice. Toss over low heat until rice turns

yellow, then add stock, parsley, salt and lemon rind. Cover and cook over very low heat for 25 minutes, or until rice is tender and stock has been absorbed. Fork in cheese and prawns, and an extra knob of butter. Heat through briefly, then serve. Serves 4.

FISH STOCK
750 g–1 kg (1³/₄–2¹/₄ lb) fish
  trimmings
1 onion, sliced
a few sprigs of parsley
1 bay leaf
pinch of salt
1 small carrot
6 black peppercorns
150 ml (1/4 pint) white wine

Place all ingredients in a saucepan, cover with water, and simmer for 30 minutes. If simmered for longer, stock could become bitter. Strain and refrigerate.

BAKED BUTTERY PRAWNS

Prawns on dinner tables are becoming as rare as hen's teeth because they're so expensive that most people reserve the pleasure of splashing out on them only when dining out. However, prawn-loving guests will be happy with just a few served as a starter, or as a light meal on a bed of savoury rice.

300 g (11 oz) fairly large,
  unshelled prawn tails (about
  24), cut and deveined
45 g (1¹/₂ oz) butter
25 ml (5 tsp) olive oil
4 large cloves garlic, crushed
25 ml (5 tsp) lemon juice
1.25 ml (1/4 tsp) paprika
25 ml (5 tsp) finely chopped
  parsley
3–4 slim spring onions,
  chopped
15 ml (1 tbsp) brandy
twisted lemon slices
  to garnish

Thaw prawns if frozen, and pat dry on paper towels. Place remaining ingredients, except lemon slices, in a 20 cm (8 in) baking dish and heat through at 200 °C (400 °F, gas 6) for about 5 minutes until butter has melted. Stir to combine, then add prawns, turning to coat on both sides. Cover securely and bake for 15 minutes. Serve immediately as suggested, with buttery juices poured over each serving, and garnish with twisted lemon slices. Hand salt and pepper mills at the table.
Serves 4 (6 prawns per person).

☆ Provide small bowls of iced water with slices of lemon for rinsing fingers.

SAUCY SQUID

My favourite squid dish, and quite different from the usual way of treating squid. This recipe disproves the theory that long, slow cooking toughens them. Very gentle simmering, with acid ingredients such as wine and tomatoes, results in butter-soft squid in a bright and bountiful sauce. The addition of canned mussels or clams adds to the seafood flavour, and the result is a creamy, savoury stew which is quite memorable served on rice or pasta, with a green salad.

45 ml (3 tbsp) sunflower oil
a nut of butter
2 large onions, finely chopped
1 kg (2¼ lb) cleaned squid tubes, sliced into thin rings
30 ml (2 tbsp) warmed brandy
75 ml (5 tbsp) medium-dry white wine
400 g (14 oz) canned tomatoes, finely chopped, plus all the juice
2.5 ml (½ tsp) salt
2.5 ml (½ tsp) paprika
5 ml (1 tsp) sugar
2 bay leaves
2.5 ml (½ tsp) dried dill
100 ml (7 tbsp) chopped parsley
225 g (8 oz) canned mussels in brine or 300 g (11 oz) canned clams in brine, drained
60 ml (4 tbsp) cultured soured cream
about 30 ml (2 tbsp) cornflour

Heat oil and butter in a large frying pan. Add onions and sauté until golden. Add squid and toss over medium heat until it stiffens and turns white. Flame (see box alongside) with brandy, shaking pan until flames die down. Add wine, tomatoes, salt, paprika, sugar, bay leaves, dill and parsley. Bring to the boil, stirring to mix. Cover and simmer over very low heat for about 1 hour, stirring occasionally, until squid is very tender and a good gravy has formed. (As it simmers, your kitchen will be filled with the most mouth-watering aroma, and after you have made the dish a few times, you will be able to tell at exactly what stage it is cooked to perfection.) Remove the bay leaves.

Add drained mussels or clams, and gently fold in cream mixed with cornflour – amount of cornflour used will depend on how much thickening sauce needs. Heat through, and serve.
Serves 6.

FLAMING FOODS
Flaming foods with certain spirits adds to the flavour, but needs to be done with care and nowhere near an extractor fan. Heat a small amount of the spirit in a small container with a long handle (do not allow to boil). Ignite, stand back and pour the flaming spirits over the food, shaking the pan until the flames die down.

FISH BAKED IN CREAM SAUCE

Fresh tomatoes and homemade fish stock are essential to this dish. Otherwise it is undemanding, particularly as neither the fish nor the mushrooms require advance cooking – they are simply added to the tomato and soured cream sauce, and left to bake in the oven until done. The result is a tasty fork supper for informal dining. Serve with pasta or rice, to soak up the flavoursome juices, and a green salad with a lemony vinaigrette.

45 ml (3 tbsp) **sunflower oil**
15 g (¹/₂ oz) **butter**
2 medium **onions**, sliced into thin rings
60 ml (4 tbsp) **flour**
5 ml (1 tsp) **paprika**
375 ml (13 fl oz) **fish stock** (see box, page 46)
400 g (14 oz) ripe **tomatoes**, skinned and finely chopped
20 ml (4 tsp) **tomato purée**

250 ml (8 fl oz) **cultured soured cream**
5 ml (1 tsp) **salt**
5 ml (1 tsp) **sugar**
750 g (1³/₄ lb) cubes of firm, filleted and skinned **fish** (such as cod)
250 g (9 oz) white **mushrooms**, wiped and thinly sliced
30 ml (2 tbsp) **medium-dry sherry**

Heat oil and butter in a large frying pan, add onions and sauté until golden. Sprinkle in flour and paprika, and when absorbed add stock, tomatoes, tomato purée, soured cream, salt and sugar. Stir until sauce thickens. Add fish, mushrooms and sherry, and mix gently. (The sauce will be very thick, but the fish and mushrooms will add juices as they bake.)
  Turn into a large, buttered baking dish, cover and bake at 180 °C (350 °F, gas 4) for 30–40 minutes.
Serves 6.

BAKED FISH AND VEGETABLES WITH GREMOLADA

Fish fillets are briefly pan-fried and then baked in a vegetable sauce with a tot of vermouth. Normally the garlicky, lemony gremolada is sprinkled on top of a finished dish, but in this recipe it is baked. If counting calories, serve with a green salad; if not, with buttered noodles, or rice tossed with lightly fried mushrooms. Use firm fillets of equal thickness, and slim courgettes. The ratio of ingredients in the gremolada may be altered to taste.

30 ml (2 tbsp) **flour**
5 ml (1 tsp) **salt**
1.25 ml (¹/₄ tsp) **paprika**
4 pieces filleted and skinned **fish** (about 675 g (1¹/₂ lb))
15 g (¹/₂ oz) **butter**
15 ml (1 tbsp) **sunflower oil**
400 g (14 oz) **courgettes**, pared and thinly sliced

1 large bunch of **spring onions**, chopped
3 large, ripe **tomatoes**, skinned and chopped (about 400 g (14 oz))
75 ml (5 tbsp) white **vermouth**
2.5 ml (¹/₂ tsp) dried **dill**

GREMOLADA
100 ml (7 tbsp) chopped **parsley**
2 cloves **garlic**, crushed
finely grated **rind** of half a medium **lemon**

Mix flour, salt and paprika, and use to dust fish lightly on both sides. Heat butter and oil in a large frying pan and fry fish briefly on both sides, in two batches. Do not cook through – you just want to seal in flavour. Arrange fish in a single layer in baking dish and set aside. Add a little extra oil to pan and add courgettes, spring onions, tomatoes, vermouth and dill. Toss to mix, then cover and simmer over very low heat for about 15

minutes, stirring occasionally, until courgettes are soft and tomatoes pulpy. On no account should mixture boil rapidly, or sauce will become dry and tacky. Pour sauce over fish.

Mix ingredients for gremolada and sprinkle over dish. Cover and bake, on middle shelf of oven, at 200 °C (400 °F, gas 6) for 20 minutes, or until fish is just cooked through.

Serves 4.

FILLETS OF FISH IN A PARCEL

This is a novel way of serving fish, and a marvellous idea for a dinner party. There is absolutely no advance cooking involved – the fish, vegetables and garlic butter are simply wrapped in sheets of greaseproof paper (which is so much more attractive than foil), refrigerated (if you wish) until just before dinner,

and then baked. The paper puffs up like filo pastry, and each diner is served with a billowing parcel on his or her plate.

The fish and flavourings you use may be altered to taste, but there are two important rules that must be followed. Firstly, greaseproof (not waxed) paper must be used. This is the paper used for lining baking trays, making icing bags and so on, and is sold in rolls of different sizes. Secondly, the fish must be patted absolutely dry before using, so that no water seeps out onto the paper, making it soggy and liable to tear. It is especially important to remember this if you are using fish that has been frozen and thawed. As the fish and vegetables are baked together, with just a little butter, the result is a purity of flavours without an excess of calories. Those on a diet will enjoy their parcels just as they are; for others, pass a jug of hot lemon-butter to pour over the contents, or a dollop of lemony mayonnaise to serve on the side.

6 x 175–200 g (6–7 oz) fish
   fillets, skinned (e.g. salmon)
30 ml (2 tbsp) lemon juice
30 ml (2 tbsp) soy sauce
250 g (9 oz) button
   mushrooms, wiped and sliced
1 bunch of spring onions plus
   some green tops, chopped
150–200 g (5–7 oz) courgettes,
   pared and coarsely grated
60 g (2 oz) butter
2–3 cloves garlic, crushed
30 ml (2 tbsp) toasted sesame
   seeds
60 ml (4 tbsp) finely chopped
   parsley
2.5 ml (½ tsp) salt

For each parcel you need one sheet of greaseproof paper measuring 45 x 35 cm (18 x 14 in) plus a smaller square to place in the middle, just under the fish, as a precaution against leaks. Brush squares with oil, and arrange one fillet in the centre of each. Sprinkle each fillet with 5 ml (1 tsp) of both lemon juice and soy sauce. Top with mush-

rooms, spring onions and courgettes, dividing equally. Cream butter with remaining ingredients, divide into six pats and place one on top of each serving. Fold paper, rolling over sides to middle first. Pinch securely to close, and then fold and pinch both ends. (They will look rather like large Cornish pasties.) Place well apart on two baking trays and, if preparing ahead, refrigerate until ready to bake.

Bake at 220 °C (425 °F, gas 7) for about 25 minutes, until paper is puffed up and lightly browned. (Exact baking time depends on thickness of fish and position in oven, but it is better to allow an extra 5 minutes rather than risk undercooked fish, especially if parcels have been refrigerated.) Using a large spatula, transfer parcels to warmed plates. The parcels may either be opened at the top, or simply lifted up – usually the contents will exit from the bottom!

Serves 6.

CHICKEN THIGHS

Chicken thighs have succulent and tender meat, but they can be very fatty, and so in many dishes using thighs, I remove the skin before cooking, leaving only a few blobs of fat here and there. The skin is easily pulled off in one piece, flavours are able to penetrate the meat, and there is no danger of ending up with a greasy gravy. Some butchers trim chicken thighs quite beautifully, removing excess skin as well as blobs of fat. Others simply tuck the lot underneath, and leave you to cut it away, resulting in a reduction in the weight you thought you had in hand. So choose your butcher — and your chicken — with care.

MOROCCAN CHICKEN

Spices play an important part in Moroccan cuisine and in the following dish they add an exotic tang to chicken. Couscous would be a fitting accompaniment, but if served with Minted Bulgur Pilaff (see page 84), a green salad and a bowl of Bulgarian yoghurt, it is tastier by far. The intriguing combination of flavours in this meal, plus the ease of preparation, make it a hot favourite. It is best cooked the day before and refrigerated overnight.

45 ml (3 tbsp) sunflower oil
1 kg (2¼ lb) skinned chicken
   thighs
2 medium onions, chopped
3 cloves garlic, crushed
2 sticks cinnamon
6 whole cloves
5 ml (1 tsp) each paprika,
   turmeric and ground ginger
7.5 ml (1½ tsp) ground cumin
10 ml (2 tsp) ground coriander
400 g (14 oz) canned tomatoes,
   chopped, plus the juice
125 ml (4 fl oz) chicken stock
5 ml (1 tsp) salt
2.5 ml (½ tsp) sugar
60 g (2 oz) seedless raisins
finely grated rind of 1 medium
   lemon

Heat half oil and lightly fry chicken in batches, on both sides, until just sealed – do not brown. Arrange in a large baking dish to fit snugly, without overlapping. Heat remaining oil in pan, add onions and soften over low heat. Add garlic and all spices, and sizzle for 1–2 minutes. Add remaining ingredients, except lemon rind, and pour over chicken. Cover and bake at 160 °C (325 °F, gas 3) for 1 hour.

If preparing in advance, remove chicken from oven, cool and refrigerate overnight. When needed, bring dish to room temperature, unless you're using a refrigerator-to-oven dish. Sprinkle lemon rind over and moisten with a little extra chicken stock. Bake, uncovered, at 160 °C (325 °F, gas 3) for 30 minutes.

If not working ahead, sprinkle with lemon rind, then bake, uncovered, for a further 15 minutes, by which time chicken should be tender and the gravy slightly reduced and thickened.

Remove cinnamon sticks and cloves before serving.
Serves 5.

HINT
The ingredients for this recipe can easily be doubled. Use two baking dishes.

☆ Buy dried herbs and spices in small quantities and keep tightly sealed in glass containers. Even then their fragrance will dissipate if kept for any length of time.

THE SIMPLEST STIR-FRIED CHICKEN

While the chicken is marinating you can prepare the vegetables and cook the rice. The stir-frying is quickly completed, making this an ideal, informal meal for the busy cook. Serve on brown or white rice.

500 g (18 oz) skinned, filleted chicken breasts
45 ml (3 tbsp) sweet sherry
25 ml (5 tsp) soy sauce
1 walnut-sized knob root ginger
2 cloves garlic, crushed
7.5–10 ml (1½–2 tsp) dark sesame oil
45 ml (3 tbsp) sunflower oil
1 red or yellow pepper, cored, seeded and diced
250 g (9 oz) brown mushrooms, wiped and sliced
4 medium carrots, thinly julienned
1 bunch of spring onions, chopped, or 2 leeks, thinly sliced
2 sticks celery plus some leaves, chopped
pinch of salt
250 ml (8 fl oz) chicken stock
25 ml (5 tsp) cornflour
toasted, slivered almonds for garnish

Slice chicken into thin strips across grain, and place in a large, shallow glass dish. Add sherry, half the soy sauce, ginger, garlic and sesame oil. Toss well to mix, then cover and stand for 1 hour.

Heat half the sunflower oil in a large frying pan or wok, add chicken strips and stir-fry briefly over medium heat, tossing constantly, until just cooked. Test by checking centre of one strip – it should be white, not pink. Remove chicken from pan, using a slotted spoon, and set aside.

Reduce heat, add remaining oil to pan, together with all vegetables, and stir-fry briefly until just softened and slightly reduced in bulk. Season lightly with salt. Return chicken to pan, add stock mixed with remaining soy sauce and cornflour, stirring until thickened.

Turn into a warmed serving dish, scatter with toasted almonds, and serve.
Serves 4–5.

STUFFED ROAST TURKEY

A favourite way of treating the Christmas turkey. The stuffings make a lovely change from the usual chestnut or sausage meat, and slow-roasting ensures a succulent bird, lightly glazed towards the end to ensure a rich brown gloss. This is an easy method of cooking turkey, leaving the cook free to attend to the rest of the festive meal. Here I have used a self-basting bird, available frozen and in different sizes at many supermarkets.

1 x 5 kg (11 lb) turkey
1 onion, chopped

GIBLET STOCK
turkey neck, gizzards and heart (not liver)
1.25 litres (2 pints) salted water
1 carrot
1 onion, halved
2 bay leaves
a few sprigs parsley

RICE, PINEAPPLE AND NUT STUFFING
200 g (7 oz) cooked rice, preferably brown
60 g (2 oz) seedless raisins
4 rings canned pineapple, drained and diced
60 g (2 oz) chopped, toasted pecan nuts
half a bunch of spring onions, chopped
25 ml (5 tsp) soy sauce
2.5 ml (½ tsp) ground ginger
1 egg, lightly beaten

SHERRIED MUSHROOM STUFFING
25 ml (5 tsp) sunflower oil
30g (1 oz) butter
1 onion, chopped
2.5 ml (½ tsp) dried thyme
125 g (4 oz) brown mushrooms, wiped and sliced
45 ml (3 tbsp) sweet sherry
125 g (4 oz) fine, fresh breadcrumbs, preferably brown
45 ml (3 tbsp) chopped parsley
salt and milled black pepper
about 75 ml (5 tbsp) reserved giblet stock

GLAZE
30 ml (2 tbsp) pale, thin honey
25 ml (5 tsp) orange-flavoured liqueur
5 ml (1 tsp) lemon juice
5 ml (1 tsp) Dijon mustard

Thaw turkey completely in the refrigerator – a 5 kg (11 lb) turkey will take about 36 hours. Remove plastic bag and legs from metal hock, following instructions on wrapper. Remove giblets and neck. Rinse turkey, inside and out, and giblets, with vinegar-water. Dry turkey well and set aside. Spoon stuffings in just before roasting.

To make giblet stock, place all ingredients in a saucepan, and simmer for 1½ hours. Strain stock and reserve.

Mix ingredients for rice stuffing and use to stuff body cavity.

To make mushroom and bread stuffing, heat oil and butter, add onion and thyme and allow to soften slowly. Add mushrooms and when beginning to shrink, add sherry, then cook until moisture has evaporated. Remove from hob and mix in breadcrumbs, parsley and seasoning, and add 75 ml (5 tbsp) of reserved stock to moisten. Handle lightly so as not to make it doughy, and use to stuff neck cavity – the breast should puff out, round and plump.

Return legs to metal hock and secure neck flap and wings with string – do not pull it tightly as the aim is simply to prevent any stuffing from escaping, and the wings from flailing sideways. Season turkey and place on a rack in a large roasting tin, breast side up. Brush with a little oil and add a little of the reserved stock or water, and onion to roasting tin. (Remember to add more liquid to roasting tin as it evaporates.)

Roast at 160 °C (325 °F, gas 3) for 3 hours, or until richly browned – there is no need to baste. Cover breast loosely with buttered paper, then roast for

another 1 1/2 hours, or until the juices in leg joint run clear when deepest part of joint is pricked.

Transfer turkey to a serving platter, mix ingredients for glaze, pour over turkey and return to oven. Make a gravy from juices in the roasting tin and remaining giblet stock. Place turkey in warming drawer or turn off oven and leave for about 15 minutes before carving.
Serves about 10.

MUSTARD-TARRAGON CHICKEN

Baked with a coating of mustard, tarragon and lemon-flavoured mayonnaise, these thighs are simply super. As there is no gravy with this chicken, serve it with a moist rice dish – either Spanish Rice or Mushroom Rice – and a crisp green salad.

1 kg (2 1/4 lb) chicken thighs, trimmed of excess fat
60 ml (4 tbsp) thick mayonnaise
15 ml (1 tbsp) pale, thin honey
25 ml (5 tsp) wholegrain mustard
5 ml (1 tsp) dried tarragon, crushed between the fingers
2.5 ml (1/2 tsp) salt
5 ml (1 tsp) finely grated lemon rind

Place chicken, skin-side up, in glass or porcelain baking dish to fit snugly. Mix remaining ingredients and spread over chicken. Stand at room temperature for 1 hour, or refrigerate for up to 4 hours, using a refrigerator-to-oven baking dish, or returning dish to room temperature before baking.

Bake, uncovered, at 160 °C (325 °F, gas 3) for 1 1/4 hours, or until richly coloured and tender. Spoon juices over each serving.
Serves 4–6.

SPICY CHICKEN SALAD

Similar to the old favourite, Coronation Chicken, but with a new twist to the spices. Poached chicken is folded into a creamy, subtly flavoured dressing. It is a great choice for a cold buffet, as it is prepared in advance and can be made in quantity. Serve with a rice or lentil salad, and fruity sambals.

1 kg (2 1/4 lb) skinned, filleted chicken breasts
3 star anise
1 onion, finely chopped
a little chopped parsley
toasted, slivered almonds for garnish

SAUCE
15 ml (1 tbsp) sunflower oil
a nut of butter
1 onion, chopped
5 ml (1 tsp) each curry power, ground coriander, cumin, fennel and cinnamon
250 ml (8 fl oz) reserved chicken stock
1 bay leaf
15 ml (1 tbsp) smooth apricot jam
200 ml (7 fl oz) thick mayonnaise
200 ml (7 fl oz) cultured buttermilk or thick Bulgarian yoghurt

Poach chicken in enough salted water almost to cover, with star anise, onion and parsley, until just tender. Cool in stock, then slice thinly across grain. Strain stock and reserve. Heat oil and butter, and sauté onion lightly. Add all spices and sizzle for 1 minute. Add reserved stock, bay leaf and jam, and simmer, uncovered, for 15 minutes, or until sauce is well reduced and syrupy. Push through a sieve; cool. Gently stir into mayonnaise mixed with buttermilk or yoghurt. Fold in chicken, and chill. Garnish with almonds.
Serves 8.

CHICKEN SALAD WITH RICE AND ALMONDS

Chicken salads are prime choices when planning a party buffet. It is comforting, however, to have a fairly basic and proven recipe to start with, and this is where the following will come in useful. It requires no outlandish items, and only a modest amount of chicken. Additional extras such as pineapple and bean sprouts supplement it deliciously, and the result is a jumbo combination of tasty things.

500–575 g (18 oz–1¼ lb) skinned, filleted chicken breasts
150 ml (¼ pint) sunflower oil
10 ml (2 tsp) dark sesame oil
2 bunches of spring onions, chopped
2 red peppers, cored, seeded and sliced into short, thin strips

2 walnut-sized knobs root ginger, peeled and finely chopped
500 g (18 oz) brown mushrooms, wiped and thinly sliced
6 thin rings fresh pineapple, finely diced
100 ml (3½ fl oz) sweet sherry
45 ml (3 tbsp) soy sauce
600 g (1¼ lb) cooked white or brown rice
125 g (4 oz) mung bean sprouts
about 100 ml (3½ fl oz) reserved chicken stock
100 g (3½ oz) toasted, slivered almonds

Poach chicken gently in salted water to half cover, with 1 chopped onion, a little parsley, 1 diced carrot and 2 bay leaves for about 10 minutes, or until just cooked. Cool in stock, then slice chicken thinly across grain. Strain stock and reserve.
Heat oils in a large frying pan, and soften spring onions, red peppers and ginger. (Keep heat

low throughout cooking period to retain all juices.) Add mushrooms and pineapple, and toss until softening. Add sherry and soy sauce, allow to bubble briefly, then tip mixture into a large bowl. Fork in rice (do not use a spoon), sliced chicken, bean sprouts and just enough reserved stock (which should have jelled) to moisten. Cool, cover and leave at room temperature for about 1 hour, or chill until required. Check seasoning for extra salt or a pinch of sugar. Fork in the toasted almonds just before serving with a large green salad tossed with a lemony French dressing and toasted sesame seeds.
Serves 10–12.

VARIATION
For extra flavour, boil rice in lightly seasoned chicken stock instead of water, with the addition of 10 ml (2 tsp) mixed dried herbs.

CRUMBED MUSTARD CHICKEN

With their coating of mustard-flavoured mayonnaise, bread-crumbs and sesame seeds, these chicken pieces are splendid served hot or cold.

100 ml (3½ fl oz) mayonnaise
30 ml (2 tbsp) wholegrain mustard
1 kg (2¼ lb) chicken thighs, skinned
100 g (3½ oz) dried breadcrumbs
45 ml (3 tbsp) sesame seeds
5 ml (1 tsp) salt
a little melted butter (optional)

Mix mayonnaise and mustard, and coat chicken thoroughly on all sides. This is best done by holding the joint at one end and spreading the mixture over thickly, using the back of a

spoon. Combine breadcrumbs, sesame seeds and salt on a large plate, then roll each chicken thigh in the mixture until thoroughly coated. (If crumbs are very fine you can expect to have some of this mixture left over – it is not necessary to use it all.) Chill chicken for at least 1 hour for crumbs to set.

To bake, arrange slightly apart in an oiled baking dish. For extra succulence, drizzle each piece with a little melted butter. Bake, uncovered, at 160 °C (325 °F, gas 3) for 1¼ hours, until tender and golden-brown.
Serves 4–6.

CHICKEN AND MANGO SALAD

A salad of pineapple and rice adds the final touch to these chicken breasts poached in apple juice, combined with mangoes and coated with a creamy curry dressing. Make both dishes in advance and refrigerate overnight.

500–575 g (18 oz–1¼ lb) skinned, filleted chicken breasts
250 ml (8 fl oz) apple juice
2 whole cloves
5 ml (1 tsp) salt
1 stick cinnamon
500 g (18 oz) fibreless mangoes, peeled and diced
chopped walnuts or pecan nuts and parsley or coriander leaves for garnish

DRESSING
25 ml (5 tsp) sunflower oil
1 medium onion, finely chopped
15 ml (1 tbsp) curry powder
5 ml (1 tsp) turmeric
125 ml (4 fl oz) reserved chicken stock
125 ml (4 fl oz) mayonnaise
125 ml (4 fl oz) cultured soured cream or thick Bulgarian yoghurt

Poach chicken gently in apple juice with cloves, salt and cinnamon for about 10 minutes, or until just cooked. Cool in stock, then slice chicken into thin strips across grain. Strain stock and reserve.

Make dressing by heating oil and softening onion, without browning. Add spices and sizzle for 1 minute. Add reserved stock and simmer, uncovered, for a few minutes until mixture thickens. Press through a sieve, discard onion, and stir sauce into mayonnaise mixed with soured cream or yoghurt. Fold chicken strips into sauce, then fold in mango. Cover and chill. Check seasoning and if too sweet, sharpen with a little lemon juice, folding it in gently. Garnish and serve with Pineapple Rice Salad (see alongside), a bowl of fresh salad leaves and a mild pawpaw chutney.
Serves 6–8.

PINEAPPLE RICE SALAD
200 g (7 oz) white long-grain rice
500 ml (17 fl oz) salted water
75 ml (5 tbsp) sunflower oil
30 ml (2 tbsp) lemon juice
5 ml (1 tsp) ground ginger
10 ml (2 tsp) pale, thin honey
1 red pepper, cored, seeded, diced and blanched (see box, page 22)
4 rings pineapple, finely diced
60 ml (4 tbsp) chopped parsley
75 ml (5 tbsp) desiccated coconut (optional)
2 medium carrots, grated
4 spring onions, chopped
sunflower seeds, if not using nuts to garnish chicken

Cook rice in salted water until dry and fluffy. Tip into a bowl. Mix oil, lemon juice, ginger and honey, and fork into hot rice. Add rest of ingredients. Cool, cover and chill.

CHICKEN WITH MUSHROOMS AND SHERRY

A time-worn old favourite, but the ingredients are so compatible that every cook should have the recipe at his or her fingertips. This version is particularly good because you do not have to reduce the sherry and then add a lot of cream to make up the sauce. Thickening a sauce with flour or cornflour is fortunately no longer taboo, which means you can use it with stock as a basis for the gravy, and then add cream modestly rather than wantonly. The touch of fresh rosemary tucked inside these breasts adds to the harmonious mixture of flavours.

2 cloves garlic, crushed
45 ml (3 tbsp) finely chopped parsley
2.5 ml (½ tsp) salt
10 ml (2 tsp) finely chopped fresh rosemary needles

6 skinned, filleted chicken breasts (about 675 g (1½ lb))
25 ml (5 tsp) sunflower oil
15 g (½ oz) butter
1 medium onion, finely chopped
250 g (9 oz) white mushrooms, wiped and sliced
10 ml (2 tsp) soy sauce
30 ml (2 tbsp) flour
300 ml (½ pint) chicken stock
60 ml (4 tbsp) medium-dry sherry
125 ml (4 fl oz) cultured soured cream

Mix garlic, parsley, salt and rosemary. Cut a neat slit in the side of each breast, taking care not to cut right through, then open out gently like the pages of a book, and sprinkle garlic mixture inside, dividing equally. Pinch breasts to close – there is no need to skewer them.

Heat oil and butter in a large frying pan, and quickly seal breasts for a few seconds on each side, without browning. Remove from pan and set aside. Add onion to pan and sauté briefly, adding an extra dash of oil if necessary. Add mushrooms and toss until just softening, then stir in soy sauce, keeping heat low to avoid scorching. When browned and well mixed, sprinkle in flour, then slowly stir in the stock. When thickened, add sherry and soured cream. Return breasts to pan – they should fit in a single layer – cover, and simmer very gently until just cooked through, about 10 minutes. Remember that even when cooked in a sauce, breasts can dry out and toughen if heat is too high. If the sauce needs reducing, tilt lid of pan very slightly while simmering. Serve with tagliatelle or brown rice.
Serves 6.

GREEK CHICKEN

This dish is simply a riot of flavours in which I have used vegetables, herbs and spices commonly used in Greek cooking with generous abandon. The result is dramatically bold and zesty, definitely not for the faint-hearted, but spot on for guests with exploratory tastes. Tie up the theme with a Greek salad, pasta or fluffy white rolls, and a fruity red wine.

25 ml (5 tsp) olive oil
1 kg (2¼ lb) well-trimmed chicken portions, preferably thighs and drumsticks
salt and milled black pepper
2 medium onions, chopped
3 cloves garlic, crushed
5 ml (1 tsp) dried oregano
2.5 ml (½ tsp) dried basil
400 g (14 oz) ripe tomatoes, skinned and chopped (not canned)
45 ml (3 tbsp) flour
125 ml (4 fl oz) chicken stock

15 ml (1 tbsp) tomato purée
2 sticks cinnamon
4 whole cloves
2 bay leaves
100 ml (7 tbsp) chopped
 parsley
5 ml (1 tsp) each salt and sugar
400 g (14 oz) aubergines, cut
 into small cubes and
 dégorged (see box, page 82)
pinch of ground cinnamon

Heat oil in a frying pan and brown chicken, skin-side first, to release any fat. Remove chicken and arrange in a single layer in a 30 x 20 cm (12 x 18 in) baking dish. (Use a fairly large dish to allow for the chunky sauce.) Season very lightly.

To pan drippings, add onions, garlic and herbs, and sauté over low heat. Add tomatoes, sprinkle in flour, then stir in stock. When thickened, add remaining ingredients, except cinnamon. Bring to the boil, stirring, then spread over chicken. Mixture will be thick, but thins out while baking.

Sprinkle lightly with cinnamon.
 Cover and bake at 160 °C (325 °F, gas 3) for 1 hour 20 minutes. Remove cinnamon sticks, bay leaves and cloves, if possible, before serving.
Serves 4–5.

CHICKEN CURRY WITH COFFEE AND COCONUT CREAM

Recipes for chicken in a curried cream sauce abound – and most of them turn out more or less the same. This one, however, has the unusual inclusion of coffee which, together with the rich coconut cream, adds colour and a flavour so subtle that it is almost indefinable, but which should nevertheless intrigue discerning diners. Serve on rice, with side dishes of sliced bananas and chutney, and a green salad with a lemony dressing.

400 ml (14 fl oz) milk
90 g (3 oz) desiccated coconut
575 g (1¼ lb) skinned, filleted
 chicken breasts
25 ml (5 tsp) sunflower oil
15 g (½ oz) butter
5 ml (1 tsp) salt
1 large onion, finely chopped
2 cloves garlic, crushed
15 ml (1 tbsp) curry powder
2.5 ml (½ tsp) ground
 cinnamon
30 ml (2 tbsp) flour
10 ml (2 tsp) pure, instant
 coffee granules dissolved in
 500 ml (17 fl oz) water
30 ml (2 tbsp) chutney
5 ml (1 tsp) pale, thin honey

Rinse saucepan with cold water to prevent milk catching. Very slowly, bring milk, coconut and a pinch of salt to the boil, stirring occasionally. Remove from hob and leave to cool. Press through a sieve, using a wooden spoon. You should have 250 ml (8 fl oz) of flavoured milk.

Slice each fillet into four thin strips – easiest if they are slightly frozen, but thaw before cooking. Heat oil and butter and quickly seal chicken on all sides, without browning. Remove from pan, season with salt and set aside.

Add onion and garlic to pan, with a little extra oil if necessary, and soften over low heat. Sprinkle in curry powder and cinnamon. (Keep heat very low, or cinnamon will scorch – a dash of water will prevent this.) Stir in flour, then diluted coffee, chutney, coconut milk and honey, bring to the boil, and then simmer, uncovered, for a few minutes, until slightly reduced, thickened and toffee-coloured. Return chicken to pan, cover and simmer very gently for about 15 minutes, or until cooked. Check seasoning – add a dash of lemon juice, if necessary. A spoon or two of the squeezed-dried coconut may also be stirred in.
Serves 4.

SIMPLE SAUCY CHICKEN

Marinated in a zesty sauce, and then left to bake, this is an easy way of treating chicken pieces. They turn out browned and succulent, with sufficient sauce to serve with rice, or with baked potatoes and soured cream flavoured with chives.

1 kg (2¹/₄ lb) chicken portions
  (halved if large)
30 ml (2 tbsp) tomato sauce
15 ml (1 tbsp) Worcestershire
  sauce
25 ml (5 tsp) smooth
  apricot jam
10 ml (2 tsp) curry powder
5 ml (1 tsp) each salt, ground
  ginger and cinnamon
125 ml (4 fl oz) fresh orange
  juice
1 medium onion, finely
  chopped
2 cloves garlic, crushed
25 ml (5 tsp) sunflower oil
25 ml (5 tsp) chutney

Arrange chicken, skin-side up, in a single layer in a glass or porcelain baking dish to fit without overlapping. Mix remaining ingredients, pour over chicken and marinate for 1 hour.

Turn chicken portions, cover, and bake at 160 °C (325 °F, gas 3) for 50 minutes. Turn again and bake, uncovered, for 30–40 minutes, until chicken is tender and golden brown, and sauce slightly thickened and reduced.
Serves 4–6.

SPICY CHICKEN PILAFF

A superb and aromatic light meal.

4 filleted, skinned chicken
  breasts (about 400 g (14 oz))
1 chicken stock cube
45 ml (3 tbsp) sunflower oil
2 medium onions, finely
  chopped

4 whole cloves
4 cardamom pods, lightly
  bruised
5 ml (1 tsp) ground coriander
5 ml (1 tsp) ground fennel
5 ml (1 tsp) cumin seeds
2 sticks cinnamon
2.5 ml (¹/₂ tsp) turmeric, or a
  pinch of saffron threads
  soaked in a dash of warm
  water
300 g (11 oz) quick-cooking,
  long-grain white rice
750 ml (1¹/₄ pints) reserved
  chicken stock
5 ml (1 tsp) salt
30 g (1 oz) sultanas or seedless
  raisins
about 75 g (2¹/₂ oz) toasted,
  slivered almonds
30 g (1 oz) butter
hard-boiled eggs, quartered,
  and chopped fresh coriander
  leaves or parsley for garnish

Place chicken in a saucepan with 250 ml (8 fl oz) salted water, 1 small onion, a little parsley, 1 small carrot and 1 bay leaf. Bring

to the boil and simmer, covered, over low heat for about 10 minutes, or until just cooked. Cool chicken in stock, then, using a very sharp knife, slice into thin strips across grain. Strain stock, measure, and make up to 750 ml (1¹/₄ pints) with the chicken stock cube and boiling water.

Heat oil in a large frying pan, add onions, and soften without browning. Add spices (including turmeric, if using; do not add saffron at this stage) and toss over low heat for 1–2 minutes. Add rice and toss until coated, then add 500 ml (18 fl oz) of reserved stock, saffron, if using, and salt. Stir to mix, then cover and simmer over very low heat for 15 minutes. Add remaining stock and sultanas or raisins, stir through quickly, then cover and simmer for about 10 minutes. Do not overcook – when done, rice will still be moist and glistening, not dry and fluffy. (If preparing in advance, cover and set aside at this stage.)

Remove whole spices and reheat gently, adding water if necessary, to avoid catching. Fork in chicken, almonds and butter to moisten. Turn onto warmed platter, surround with hard-boiled eggs and sprinkle with coriander or parsley.
Serves 4–6.

RAITA
500 ml (17 fl oz) thick Bulgarian yoghurt
4 spring onions, chopped
quarter of a cucumber, peeled, seeded and diced
2 small tomatoes, chopped
2 cloves garlic, crushed
pinch each of salt and sugar
5 ml (1 tsp) garam masala (or to taste)

Mix all ingredients together, cover and chill for a few hours before serving.

STUFFED CHICKEN THIGHS WITH BUTTERNUT SQUASH PURÉE

The butternut purée served alongside takes the place of gravy.

30 ml (2 tbsp) sunflower oil
1 pickling onion, finely chopped
1 clove garlic, crushed
2.5 ml (½ tsp) finely grated lemon rind
5 ml (1 tsp) fresh thyme leaves
25 ml (5 tsp) finely chopped parsley
30 g (1 oz) fine, fresh white or brown breadcrumbs
pinch of salt
10 ml (2 tsp) mayonnaise
8 chicken thighs (about 1 kg (2¼ lb))
a little French mustard, preferably tarragon-flavoured
sunflower oil for brushing
pinch each of salt and paprika

BUTTERNUT SQUASH PURÉE
500 g (18 oz) peeled and diced butternut squash
250 ml (8 fl oz) fresh orange juice
1 pickling onion, chopped
1.25 ml (¼ tsp) salt
10 ml (2 tsp) pale, thin honey
2 sticks cinnamon
a nut of butter (optional)

Heat oil and sauté onion and garlic until lightly browned. Remove from heat and add lemon rind, thyme, parsley, breadcrumbs and salt, then bind with mayonnaise. Carefully lift skin from 'straight' side of each thigh, leaving it attached at the other side. Smooth a portion of stuffing over flesh, dividing the mixture equally between the thighs. Spread underside of skin with a little mustard, then flap skin back. Skewer, or simply press to close. (If not skewered the skin tends to crimp during baking, but this is by no means a detraction.)

Arrange thighs in a single layer in a baking dish. Do not pack tightly – they should just touch. Brush with oil and season lightly with salt and paprika. Bake, uncovered, at 160 °C (325 °F, gas 3) for 1 hour 10 minutes, or until tender and browned. Transfer to warmed serving platter, discarding fat.

To make purée, place all ingredients, except butter, in a saucepan and bring to the boil. Simmer, covered, until butternut squash is soft, adding a dash of water if juice boils away too quickly. Discard cinnamon sticks, drain butternut squash if necessary and purée in a blender until smooth. Reheat, adding a nut of butter, if using.
Serves 4–6.

Before cooking, always wipe red meat and poultry (the cavity as well) with a paper towel moistened with vinegar or a vinegar-water solution.

CHICKEN SALAD WITH FRESH BASIL SAUCE

Poached chicken breasts, fanned out on a serving platter, blanketed with a creamy basil sauce and surrounded with coloured noodles – this is an elegant salad and an excellent choice for a summer luncheon party, when fresh basil abounds. Fillets of bream are also good done this way.

8–10 skinned, filleted chicken breasts (about 1 kg (2¹/₄ lb))
1 onion, chopped
a few black peppercorns
cherry tomatoes, and black olives for garnish

SAUCE
45 ml (3 tbsp) parsley sprigs
20 g (³/₄ oz) fresh basil leaves
1 clove garlic, peeled
45 ml (3 tbsp) olive oil
25 ml (5 tsp) grated Parmesan
125 ml (4 fl oz) mayonnaise
125 ml (4 fl oz) thick Bulgarian yoghurt

PASTA
500 g (18 oz) fusilli noodles
about 125 ml (4 fl oz) garlicky French dressing

First make sauce: place parsley, basil, garlic, oil and cheese in a processor fitted with grinding blade. Process to a creamy consistency, stopping once or twice to scrape down sides. In a bowl, stir mayonnaise and yoghurt together until smooth. Add basil mixture and stir, then tip into a container and chill.

Poach chicken gently in a little salted water with onion and a few black peppercorns, until just tender. Do not overcook. Cool, strain stock and reserve.

Cook pasta, drain well, toss with enough French dressing to moisten nicely, and set aside.

To assemble, arrange chicken on a serving platter. Slice each breast thinly lengthwise, leaving slices joined at base, and carefully fan them out. (This step is optional and does not apply if you're using fish.) Thin basil sauce to a pouring consistency with a little reserved stock; pour over breasts. Surround with noodles, garnish and serve.
Serves 8–10.

SLIGHTLY TIPSY CHICKEN WITH ALMONDS

A fancy title for a dish that is not at all pompous, but it does encapsulate the ingredients: a dash of brandy, a tipple of orange liqueur, and a topping of almonds, combining to give baked chicken thighs a new flavour. The preparation is speedy and straightforward.

1 kg (2¼ lb) chicken thighs, trimmed of excess fat
salt and curry powder
60 ml (4 tbsp) fresh orange juice
25 ml (5 tsp) orange liqueur
10 ml (2 tsp) brandy
2.5 ml (½ tsp) Worcestershire sauce
10 ml (2 tsp) Dijon mustard
25 ml (5 tsp) chutney
about 30 g (1 oz) white or brown breadcrumbs
toasted, slivered almonds

First place chicken, skin-side up, in a lightly oiled baking dish to fit fairly snugly. Sprinkle pieces with salt and curry powder, and rub in lightly. Bake, uncovered, at 160 °C (325 °F, gas 3) for 30 minutes.

Mix orange juice, liqueur, brandy, Worcestershire sauce, mustard, chutney, and just enough of the breadcrumbs to make a moist but spreadable paste. Spoon half this mixture over thighs, dividing equally. Return to oven and bake for a further 15 minutes. Remove from oven and spread with remaining mixture and press almonds in lightly. If insufficient juices have formed, pour in a little water or stock at side of baking dish, and return to oven for a further 15–20 minutes, until tender and browned.

Spoon any juices from the dish over each portion before serving. **Serves 4–6.**

FINGER-LICKING CHICKEN WINGS

Marinate chicken wings in a barbecue-type sauce, to add colour, flavour and versatility, then serve as an economical main course with the juices spooned over, accompanied by baked potatoes and soured cream; or drain the juices and serve with drinks; or grill over the coals and pass them round for nibbling, to appease appetites.

1 kg (2¼ lb) chicken wings
30 ml (2 tbsp) sunflower oil
45 ml (3 tbsp) sweet sherry
45 ml (3 tbsp) tomato sauce
30 ml (2 tbsp) lemon juice
5 ml (1 tsp) Worcestershire sauce
15 ml (1 tbsp) soy sauce
10 ml (2 tsp) pale, thin honey
10 ml (2 tsp) curry powder
10 ml (2 tsp) chilli sauce (or more for extra bite)
salt and freshly milled black pepper

Remove wing tips if not already done, then pull wings apart and cut through at joint, making two pieces. Do not cut through the bone, but at the precise point where the joint separates. Arrange in a single layer in a large glass or porcelain baking dish – 30 x 25 cm (12 x 10 in) is ideal.

Mix remaining ingredients, except salt and pepper, pour over wings and leave for 1 hour at room temperature; or refrigerate for up to 6 hours, turn several times. Return dish to room temperature before baking.

Season very lightly, and bake, uncovered, at 180 °C (350 °F, gas 4) for 25 minutes. Turn pieces over, and add a little water to the baking dish if necessary, to prevent scorching. Reduce heat to 160 °C (325 °F, gas 3) and bake for a further 25 minutes, or until tender, browned and juicy. **Makes about 32 pieces, serving 5–6 as a main course.**

BURGUNDY CHICKEN CASSEROLE

Unmistakably French, this delectable dish of chicken, red wine, tiny onions and mushrooms, is closely related to Coq au Vin but simpler and more peasanty, as it dispenses with the bacon, brandy and fried bread. Serve with rice or ribbon noodles and a salad.

12 pickling onions, peeled
sunflower oil
1 kg (2¹/4 lb) chicken thighs, trimmed of excess fat
2.5 ml (¹/2 tsp) each salt and paprika
1 small onion, chopped
1 red pepper, cored, seeded and diced
250 g (9 oz) brown mushrooms, wiped and sliced
2.5 ml (¹/2 tsp) dried thyme
30 ml (2 tbsp) flour
250 ml (8 fl oz) chicken stock
100 ml (3¹/2 fl oz) robust red wine
15 ml (1 tbsp) tomato purée
2.5 ml (¹/2 tsp) each salt and sugar
5 ml (1 tsp) Worcestershire sauce

Cut a cross through root end of each pickling onion. Arrange in a single layer in a saucepan, half-cover with salted cold water, add a pinch of sugar, and bring to the boil. Reduce heat and simmer for 8 minutes, then drain and set aside. (Do not boil rapidly or overcook, as onions must retain their shape.) Smear base of frying pan with a dash of sunflower oil and lightly brown chicken on both sides, skin-side first, to release fat. Arrange chicken, skin-side up, in baking dish to fit, and sprinkle with salt and paprika. Cover and bake at 160 °C (325 °F, gas 3) for 30 minutes. Meanwhile, make sauce. Add onion and red pepper to pan drippings, and sauté. Add mushrooms, thyme and a little extra oil, if necessary, and stir-fry until softened. Sprinkle in flour, tossing to mix, then add remaining ingredients, stirring until sauce thickens.

Uncover chicken; pour off fat. Pour sauce over, and tuck in parboiled pickling onions. Cover and bake for a further 45 minutes, or until chicken is tender. **Serves 4.**

HONEY CURRY CHICKEN WITH APPLE

This dish is a beauty. Exceptional in both colour and flavour, it is quite different from ordinary chicken curry. First marinated in apple juice spiked with spices, fresh apples are added to the casserole before baking. The resultant sauce, a bright nosegay of flavours, is blended to blanket the chicken.

1 kg (2¹/4 lb) chicken thighs, trimmed of excess fat
1 medium onion, chopped
2 cloves garlic, crushed
250 ml (8 fl oz) apple juice
15 ml (1 tbsp) curry powder
15 ml (1 tbsp) pale, thin honey
5 ml (1 tsp) turmeric
30 ml (2 tbsp) lemon juice
5 ml (1 tsp) ground cumin
5 star anise
2 sticks cinnamon
5 ml (1 tsp) salt
2 medium Golden Delicious apples, peeled and sliced
10-15 ml (2–3 tsp) cornflour, if necessary

Arrange chicken, skin-side down, in a glass or porcelain baking dish to fit fairly snugly. Mix onion, garlic, apple juice, curry powder, honey, turmeric, lemon juice and cumin, and pour over chicken. Tuck in star anise and cinnamon sticks, and marinate for 1–2 hours.

Turn chicken, season with salt, and add apple slices, pushing

them in wherever there is a space. Bake, covered, at 160 °C (325 °F, gas 3) for 1 hour, or until chicken is tender. Using a slotted spoon, transfer chicken to ovenproof serving platter. Cool sauce briefly, remove star anise and cinnamon sticks, then purée in a blender until smooth. If sauce is rather thin, add cornflour and blend again. Pour over chicken and return to oven for about 20 minutes, until bubbling.
Serves 4–6.

CHICKEN PORTIONS
A mini-portion pack consisting of one chicken cut into 16 pieces, is perfect for Spicy Masala Chicken. These smaller pieces cook more quickly and are less likely to crowd the pan. If you cut up the chicken yourself, try to cut through the joints, not bones, to avoid splintering.

SPICY MASALA CHICKEN

A kaleidoscope of spices goes into this balmy chicken curry. Serve with Basmati rice and fruity sambals.

3 cloves garlic, crushed
1 walnut-sized knob root ginger, peeled and chopped
30 ml (2 tbsp) sunflower oil
2 medium onions, chopped
2 sticks cinnamon
6 cardamom pods, bruised
5 ml (1 tsp) ground cumin
5 ml (1 tsp) ground coriander
2.5 ml (1/2 tsp) ground fennel
1 kg (2 1/4 lb) chicken portions
400 g (14 oz) ripe tomatoes, skinned and chopped
5 ml (1 tsp) turmeric
4 whole cloves
4 curry leaves, rinsed in salt water and soaked, or 2 bay leaves
5 ml (1 tsp) salt
large pinch of sugar
5–10 ml (1–2 tsp) garam masala
250 ml (8 fl oz) water
chopped coriander leaves or parsley for garnish

Pound together garlic and ginger in a mortar with a few drops of the oil. Set aside. Heat oil in a large frying pan and braise onions until golden brown. Reduce heat and add cinnamon, cardamom, cumin, coriander and fennel, and sizzle briefly. Add chicken, skin-side down, and brown lightly, turning once. Add remaining ingredients, then cover and simmer over very low heat for 30–40 minutes, or until chicken is cooked. Stir occasionally to mash the tomatoes. Tilt lid of pan and simmer for a further 10 minutes to reduce and thicken gravy to desired consistency. Check seasoning and remove whole spices and curry or bay leaves. Turn into warmed serving dish, and garnish.
Serves 4–6.

SAMBALS
Fiery sambals, combining raw fruit and vegetables with chillies, would usurp the gentle fragrance of the Spicy Masala Chicken, so gentler condiments are preferable. Apart from the usual sliced bananas and chopped nuts, you could use the following basic mixtures. Serve as they are, or add your own `bite' to taste.
☆ *Peeled and chopped apples, lemon juice, raisins, ground cumin, chopped spring onion, chopped walnuts and Bulgarian yoghurt.*
☆ *Pawpaw chutney, desiccated coconut and sunflower seeds.*
☆ *Diced fresh pineapple, chopped fresh mint, spring onions and Bulgarian yoghurt.*

ROAST SIRLOIN WITH MUSHROOM STUFFING

This roast has a superb flavour.

1 x 1.75 kg (4 lb) boned, rolled sirloin
salt and milled black pepper

MARINADE
45 ml (3 tbsp) soy sauce
45 ml (3 tbsp) medium-dry sherry
2 cloves garlic, crushed
1 walnut-sized knob root ginger, peeled, finely chopped

STUFFING
25 ml (5 tsp) sunflower oil
1 small onion, chopped
250 g (9 oz) white mushrooms, wiped and sliced
45 g (1½ oz) white or brown breadcrumbs
2.5 ml (½ tsp) dried thyme
45 ml (3 tbsp) beef stock

Remove strings from sirloin, open out and lay flat in a large glass dish suitable for marinating. Mix ingredients for marinade, pour over meat and leave for 2 hours, turning once.

Heat oil and lightly sauté onions and mushrooms. Remove from hob and add remaining stuffing ingredients.

Remove meat from marinade, season lightly, spread with stuffing, roll and tie, then season outside lightly. Place on a rack in a roasting tin. Add 500 ml (17 fl oz) water, 1 chopped onion and 1 bay leaf to pan. The water should not touch the meat. Pour remaining marinade over meat and roast at 160 °C (325 °F, gas 3) for 1 hour. Cover with a tent of foil, shiny side out, and roast for 1 hour 10 minutes. Stand in warming drawer for 10 minutes, then carve. Reduce gravy by boiling rapidly in a small saucepan.
Serves 8.

LAYERED SAVOURY MINCE WITH RICE AND LENTILS

A dish of curried mince tucked between layers of spicy rice and lentils. Serve in wedges, like a pie, with Bulgarian yoghurt, chutney and salads.

RICE AND LENTILS
15 ml (1 tbsp) sunflower oil
100 g (3½ oz) brown rice
100 g (3½ oz) brown or green lentils, picked over and rinsed
500 ml (17 fl oz) water
400 g (14 oz) canned tomatoes, finely chopped, plus the juice
2.5 ml (½ tsp) salt
5 ml (1 tsp) sugar
1 stick cinnamon
2 star anise
2.5 ml (½ tsp) each ground cumin, coriander and turmeric

MEAT MIXTURE
1 slice crustless bread
300 ml (½ pint) milk
25 ml (5 tsp) sunflower oil
1 medium onion, chopped
2 cloves garlic, crushed
10 ml (2 tsp) curry powder
2.5 ml (½ tsp) turmeric
1.25 ml (¼ tsp) grated nutmeg
10 ml (2 tsp) brown vinegar
25 ml (5 tsp) chutney
500 g (18 oz) minced beef
30 g (1 oz) seedless raisins
5 ml (1 tsp) salt
1 egg, beaten

CUSTARD TOPPING
1 egg
reserved milk
pinch each of salt and turmeric
45 ml (3 tbsp) desiccated coconut
a few bay leaves
garam masala

To prepare rice and lentils, pour oil onto base of a large saucepan, add rice, lentils, water, tomatoes, salt, sugar and spices, and bring

to the boil, stirring once to mix. Cover and simmer very gently for 1 hour, without stirring, or until liquid is absorbed and rice and lentils are cooked. Remove cinnamon stick and star anise, and set mixture aside.

To make meat mixture, soak bread in milk. Heat oil and fry onion and garlic. Mix in spices, vinegar and chutney. Squeeze milk from bread, reserving milk. Add bread to pan, together with mince, raisins and salt. Toss over low heat until mince is no longer pink. Remove from hob and add egg, mixing well.

To assemble, oil a deep, 23 cm (9 in) pie dish and spread half rice mixture over the base. Spoon mince mixture over in an even layer. Top with remaining rice mixture, spreading evenly.

To make custard topping, beat egg into reserved milk, add salt, turmeric and coconut, and pour evenly over the rice mixture. Insert bay leaves here and there, and dust with garam masala. To

prevent drying out, stand dish in a larger pan and add enough water to pan to reach halfway up the sides of the baking dish. Bake, uncovered, at 180 ˚C (350 ˚F, gas 4) for 1 hour.
Serves 8–10.

SLIMMER'S STROGANOFF

This title is an outright misnomer, but it does serve to catch the eye. Firstly, it is not slimming – what dish of fried steak in thick gravy can possibly be low in calories? However, it does not contain the soured cream that is an important ingredient in the traditional recipe. Secondly, it stretches a mere 575 g (1¼ lb) of fillet to serve six people. Thirdly it is quick to make, and jolly good. Serve on rice or ribbon noodles, with a crisp green salad, and hand a pepper mill at the table.

575 g (1¼ lb) fillet of beef
20 ml (4 tsp) Worcestershire sauce
3–4 cloves garlic, crushed
2.5 ml (½ tsp) dried thyme, crushed between the fingers
30 ml (2 tbsp) sunflower oil
250 g (9 oz) brown mushrooms, wiped and thinly sliced
1 large bunch of spring onions, chopped
500 ml (17 fl oz) skimmed milk
30 ml (2 tbsp) tomato purée
25 ml (5 tsp) soy sauce
pinch each of salt and sugar
20 ml (4 tsp) cornflour
45 ml (3 tbsp) medium-dry sherry

Slice beef across grain into wafer-thin strips, measuring about 6 x 1 cm (2½ x ½ in). This is most easily done if beef is semi-frozen. Place in a large, shallow dish, add Worcestershire sauce, garlic and thyme, toss to mix, then cover loosely and marinate for 45 minutes.

Heat oil in a large frying pan and stir-fry steak briefly, until just browned, tossing constantly. Add mushrooms and spring onions, and keep tossing, over medium heat, until softening. Turn heat to very low and add milk, tomato purée, soy sauce, salt and sugar. Stir to mix, then cover and simmer very gently for 4–5 minutes.

Mix cornflour with sherry, stir into pan, and allow to boil up, stirring, until sauce has smoothed and thickened.
Serves 6.

CHILLI-GLAZED MEAT LOAF

When it emerges from the oven, this loaf could almost be mistaken for a richly browned roast. Unlike most meat loaves, it is not baked in a tin, but patted into a loaf shape and spread with a zesty sauce before baking. The result is a tasty way of serving mince in a new guise.

500 g (18 oz) lean minced beef
1 egg, lightly beaten
1 slice crustless white or brown bread, crumbled
60 ml (4 tbsp) chopped parsley
1 large onion, finely chopped
5 ml (1 tsp) salt
5 ml (1 tsp) mixed dried herbs

SAUCE
30 ml (2 tbsp) chilli sauce*
25 ml (5 tsp) tomato sauce
5 ml (1 tsp) Worcestershire sauce
10 ml (2 tsp) light brown sugar
10 ml (2 tsp) mayonnaise

Combine ingredients for meat loaf thoroughly and shape into a loaf measuring about 20 x 7.5 cm (8 x 3 in). Place in centre of a shallow, oiled baking dish that is large enough to take loaf without having it touch sides.

Mix ingredients for sauce and spread over top and sides of loaf, allowing it to trickle down. Bake at 160 °C (325 °F, gas 3) for 30 minutes, then add a little water to dish, pouring it round loaf. This will prevent glaze from scorching, and will also provide some juicy gravy, but add it sparingly as it is better to add a little more later on, if necessary. Bake for a further 30 minutes, basting once with juices in dish. Slice and serve with the gravy.
Serves 6.

* The chilli sauce I use is a thick, hot and spicy sauce that includes tomato purée, vinegar and sugar, and may be used as a condiment as well as for cooking.

GOURMET BEEF AND BUTTER BEAN CASSEROLE

When the weather is chilly, a satisfying stew is comforting. The following recipe is a little more sophisticated than usual, with brandy, wine, pickling onions and mushrooms adding a touch of French flair. If, however, you wish to delete the French flair, refer to the variation at the end. Serve either with pearl barley or buttered noodles and a green vegetable.

1 kg (2¼ lb) boned shoulder braising steak, or thick flank, cubed
60 ml (4 tbsp) sunflower oil
20 g (¾ oz) butter
30 ml (2 tbsp) warmed brandy
2 medium onions, chopped
4 cloves garlic, crushed
4 medium carrots, diced
10 ml (2 tsp) dried tarragon, crushed between the fingers
250 ml (8 fl oz) tomato passata
250 ml (8 fl oz) red wine
500 ml (17 fl oz) beef stock
5 ml (1 tsp) salt
10 ml (2 tsp) brown sugar
16 small pickling onions
250 g (9 oz) brown mushrooms, wiped and finely chopped
2 x 400 g (14 oz) cans butter beans, drained
chopped parsley for garnish

Pat beef dry on paper towels. Heat half oil and half butter in a very large frying pan and brown beef over high heat, adding cube by cube to avoid stewing. Flame (see box, page 47) with brandy, then transfer to a large baking dish. Reduce heat, add remaining oil and butter to pan, add onions, garlic, carrots and tarragon, and toss until softening. Add tomato passata, wine, stock and seasoning, stir until hot, then pour over beef.

Cover securely and bake at 160 °C (325 °F, gas 3) for 1 hour.

Remove from oven and stir. Bake, covered, for a further 30 minutes.

Meanwhile, peel pickling onions, nick a cross in stem end, place in a saucepan of cold water, bring to the boil and simmer for 10 minutes. Drain and fold into stew together with mushrooms and beans. If gravy has reduced too much, add a little extra stock and a tipple of red wine mixed with a little cornflour to thicken it. Cover and return to oven for 45 minutes, or until meat is butter-soft and stew is bubbling in a richly coloured gravy. Garnish and serve.
Serves 8.

VARIATION
Omit the pickling onions and mushrooms. Add the beans to the meat after 1½ hours, adding extra liquid if necessary, and return to the oven for about 15 minutes.

BEEF AND BEER CURRY WITH MACADAMIA NUTS

Certain noteworthy men had unkind words to say about beer. Bernard Shaw simply did not like it; Aristotle said it tended to stupefy. Nevertheless, a lot of people do rather like it, and cooking with beer has developed a novel appeal. This is a slightly fruity curry, lightly spiced, with macadamias adding a surprising crunch. Serve with rice, sambals and salad.

750 g (1 ¾ lb) beef topside or thick flank
30 ml (2 tbsp) sunflower oil
15 g (½ oz) butter
2 medium onions, chopped
2 cloves garlic, crushed
1 knob root ginger, peeled and finely chopped (about 10 ml (2 tsp))
15 ml (1 tbsp) curry powder
2.5 ml (½ tsp) turmeric

2 Golden Delicious apples, peeled and diced
2 sticks cinnamon
6 whole cloves
15 ml (1 tbsp) flour
300 ml (½ pint) beer
250 ml (8 fl oz) beef stock
30 ml (2 tbsp) chutney
15 ml (1 tbsp) tomato purée
5 ml (1 tsp) each salt and brown sugar
75–100 g (2½–3½ oz) coarsely chopped, toasted macadamia nuts
Bulgarian yoghurt (optional)

Cut meat into small cubes or slice into thin strips across grain, and dry well. Heat oil and butter in a large frying pan and brown meat in two batches over high heat. Transfer to a large baking dish. Reduce heat, add a little more oil to pan, and lightly fry onions, garlic, ginger, curry powder, turmeric, apples, cinnamon and cloves. Sprinkle in flour, then stir in beer, stock, chutney, tomato purée, salt and sugar.

Bring to the boil, then mix into meat. Cover securely and bake on middle shelf of oven at 160 °C (325 °F, gas 3) for 1½ hours. Remove cinnamon stick and cloves, and add macadamias. Cover (unless gravy needs reducing) and return to oven for a further 15 minutes. If using yoghurt, streak in a few spoons just before serving.
Serves 6–8.

> *When wrapping food for cooking, or covering a dish with aluminium foil prior to baking, always have the dull side towards the food and the shiny side out.*

BRAZILIAN-STYLE BEEF

A cup of coffee, a few tipsy prunes, a couple of vegetables and a touch of spice do magic things to a simple beef stew. Serve on beans, rice or barley, with a salad.

10 large dried prunes
red wine
750 g (1 3/4 lb) beef topside or thick flank
45 ml (3 tbsp) sunflower oil
2 medium onions, chopped
2 cloves garlic, crushed
4 medium carrots, julienned
250 g (9 oz) brown mushrooms, wiped and sliced
25 ml (5 tsp) flour
10 ml (2 tsp) pure, instant coffee granules
10 ml (2 tsp) pale, thin honey
250 ml (8 fl oz) hot water
250 ml (8 fl oz) beef stock
5 ml (1 tsp) salt
2.5 ml (1/2 tsp) ground mixed spice

Cover prunes with red wine and leave to soak. Slice beef into small cubes or thin strips across grain, and pat dry. Heat oil in a large frying pan and brown beef over high heat in two batches to avoid stewing. (A sprinkling of brown sugar will hasten browning.) Transfer meat to a large baking dish. Reduce heat, add a little extra oil to pan, and lightly sauté onions, garlic, carrots and mushrooms. Sprinkle in flour, then stir in coffee and honey dissolved in the hot water. Add stock, bring to the boil, then add salt and mixed spice. Mix sauce into beef.

Cover securely and bake on middle shelf of oven at 160 °C (325 °F, gas 3) for 1 1/2 hours. Sliver soaked prunes, discarding stones, and stir into stew together with some or all of the wine, depending on how much extra gravy is required. Cover and return to oven for a further 15 minutes.
Serves 6–8.

FILLET OF BEEF WITH HERB BUTTER

This is a basic recipe for one of the simplest and most popular ways of serving sliced fillet of beef. With the butter prepared in advance, this is a superb quick meal.

6–8 slices fillet of beef (about 750 g (1 3/4 lb))
soy sauce
pinch of salt
45 ml (3 tbsp) sherry (optional)

HERB BUTTER
60 g (2 oz) soft butter
1–2 cloves garlic, crushed
1 x 10 cm (4 in) sprig thyme, leaves stripped*
3 fresh sage leaves, chopped*
1 x 10 cm (4 in) sprig marjoram, leaves chopped*
25 ml (5 tsp) chopped parsley
1 slim spring onion, chopped
1.25 ml (1/4 tsp) paprika

First make herb butter: mash together all ingredients, cover and set aside.

Heat two medium or one extra-large frying pan and brush with just a slick of oil, or use non-stick pans. Brush each side of steak lightly with soy sauce and fry quickly, turning once, until done to your liking. Salt very lightly and arrange on a warmed platter. If using sherry, add it to the pan and boil rapidly until almost evaporated. Turn heat off, add the herb butter, stir to melt and heat through, then pour over the steaks and serve immediately.
Serves 6–8.

* If using dried herbs, substitute 2.5 ml (1/2 tsp) each dried thyme and marjoram for the fresh thyme, sage and marjoram. Be sure to use level measures or the flavour will be too pronounced – in the case of dried herbs, remember less is always better than more.

FILLET OF BEEF WITH PORT AND ROSEMARY SAUCE

This is an admirable way of treating fillet. It does require last-minute attention, but for a small, special-occasion dinner it is perfectly manageable, and the flavour of the sauce is memorable.

4 slices fillet of beef (500–575 g
  (18 oz–1¹/₄ lb))
1 small sprig rosemary
30 ml (2 tbsp) sunflower oil
2 cloves garlic, crushed
45 ml (3 tbsp) tawny port
5 ml (1 tsp) Dijon mustard
15 ml (1 tbsp) soy sauce*
125 ml (4 fl oz) beef stock
60 ml (4 tbsp) cultured soured
  cream

Arrange steaks in a single layer in a small glass dish, without their overlapping. Strip needles from rosemary and chop finely – rose-mary is a strongly flavoured herb and you will need just less than 5 ml (1 tsp), chopped. Mix rosemary with oil, garlic, port, mustard and soy sauce, and pour over steaks. If mustard has not dissolved, rub into steaks with the back of a spoon. Marinate for 2 hours, turning twice.

Heat a heavy-based or a non-stick frying pan and brush with a slick of oil. Fry steaks, turning once. Transfer to serving dish and keep warm. Stir stock and cream into remaining marinade, add to frying pan and heat, stirring, until brown and syrupy, about 1–2 minutes. Pour over steaks and serve immediately. **Serves 4.**

* The addition of soy sauce eliminates the need for salt, but be sure to use a light, thin soy sauce (as opposed to a thick, dark brand) to avoid scorching.

PIQUANT STEAK

Use fillet, rump or porterhouse – the marinade tenderizes, while imparting a moderately robust flavour.

4–6 beef steaks (about
  675–750 g (1¹/₂–1³/₄ lb)),
  trimmed of excess fat
25 ml (5 tsp) sunflower oil
1 large onion, finely chopped
2 cloves garlic, crushed
25 ml (5 tsp) chutney
20 ml (4 tsp) Worcestershire
  sauce
25 ml (5 tsp) tomato sauce
10 ml (2 tsp) Dijon mustard
10 ml (2 tsp) pale, thin honey
2.5 ml (¹/₂ tsp) dried oregano
15 ml (1 tbsp) red wine vinegar
salt and milled black pepper
100 ml (3¹/₂ fl oz) red wine*
60 ml (4 tbsp) cultured soured
  cream*

Arrange steaks in a shallow, glass or non-metal dish. Heat oil and sauté onion and garlic. Remove from hob and stir in chutney, Worcestershire and tomato sauce, mustard, honey, oregano and vinegar. Mix well, then spread over steaks – the mixture will be thick – and leave to marinate for about 3 hours, turning several times.

Heat a slick of oil in a heavy-based frying pan and fry steaks over medium heat until done to your liking, turning once, and seasoning as you turn. (It is important to keep heat on medium rather than high, as saucy marinades tend to scorch.)

Arrange steaks on serving platter and keep warm. Add any remaining marinade to pan, together with red wine. Reduce by rapid boiling for a few seconds, then swirl in cream. Pour over steaks and serve at once. **Serves 4–6.**

* The red wine and cream may be omitted. Add a little hot beef stock to the pan, heat to bubbling, then pour over the steaks.

CASEROLED VEAL CHOPS

Veal is a fairly neutral meat which loves being pampered with herbs, wine and vegetables, as in the following Continental-style casserole. Slowly baked in a lusty sauce, then topped with a herby gremolada, these chops turn out very tender and very tasty. Serve this robust dish with a leafy salad and pasta, or with rice tinted with saffron or turmeric for a really colourful presentation. This recipe may easily be doubled.

25 ml (5 tsp) olive oil
a nut of butter
4 veal chops (about 575 g (1¼ lb))
1 small onion, chopped
2 leeks, sliced
2 cloves garlic, crushed
1 red pepper, cored, seeded and diced
2.5 ml (½ tsp) mixed dried herbs or Herbs Provençale*

25 ml (5 tsp) flour
400 g (14 oz) canned tomatoes, chopped, plus the juice
200 g (7 oz) courgettes, pared and sliced
10 ml (2 tsp) tomato purée
2 bay leaves
60 ml (4 tbsp) chopped parsley
125 ml (4 fl oz) semi-sweet white wine
5 ml (1 tsp) each salt and sugar
sliced black olives (optional)**

GREMOLADA
30 ml (2 tbsp) chopped parsley
30 ml (2 tbsp) chopped chives
1 clove garlic, crushed
5 ml (1 tsp) finely grated lemon rind
6 large fresh basil leaves, chopped

Heat oil and butter and brown chops lightly on both sides. Transfer to a 20 x 20 x 5 cm (8 x 8 x 2 in) baking dish. Reduce heat, add onion, leeks, garlic, red pepper and herbs to pan, and stir-fry briefly. Sprinkle in flour, stir until absorbed, then add remaining ingredients, except olives. Bring to the boil, then pour over chops.

Cover and bake at 160 °C (325 °F, gas 3) for 1¼ hours. Stir in olives. If gravy needs reducing, remove cover before baking for a further 15 minutes. Remove bay leaves.

Mix ingredients for gremolada, sprinkle over casserole, and bake for a further 10–15 minutes, until just bubbling.
Serves 4.

* Herbs Provençale usually comprise dried rosemary, marjoram, savory, oregano, basil and tarragon.

** Black olives are used as they provide a colour contrast. The main difference between black and green olives is that the former have been ripened.

CREAMY VEAL PAPRIKA

Soured cream, mushrooms and paprika are a favourite sauce combination, used here in a simple goulash. Ladle over spinach noodles or serve on rice. Top with toasted almonds on smarter occasions.

25 ml (5 tsp) sunflower oil
15 g (½ oz) butter
2 medium onions, chopped
2 red or yellow peppers, cored, seeded and diced
1 kg (2¼ lb) stewing veal, cut into small cubes
pinch of salt
45 ml (3 tbsp) flour
10 ml (2 tsp) paprika
500 ml (17 fl oz) chicken stock
250 g (9 oz) white mushrooms, wiped and thinly sliced
125 ml (4 fl oz) cultured soured cream
30 ml (2 tbsp) medium-dry sherry
15 fresh sage leaves, chopped

finely chopped parsley, or
 chopped, toasted almonds
 for garnish

Heat oil and butter and sauté
onions and peppers. Transfer to a
large baking dish. Pat veal dry,
add to pan in batches to avoid
stewing, and toss until golden
brown, adding extra oil as necessary. Transfer to dish with
onions; salt lightly. Stir flour and
paprika into pan drippings, then
slowly stir in stock. When thickened, pour over veal. Cover
securely and bake at 160 ˚C
(325 ˚F, gas 3) for 1½ hours, or
until veal is tender. Remove from
oven and stir in mushrooms,
soured cream, sherry and sage.
Return to oven, uncovered, for
20 minutes, or until mushrooms
are cooked. Check seasoning – it
may need a pinch of salt or
sugar. Turn into a large, warmed
dish, surround with noodles or
rice, and garnish.
Serves 6.

GLAZED LEG OF LAMB WITH ROSEMARY

*You must have fresh rosemary for
this dish. It is the ultimate herb to
use with lamb and in the following
recipe it provides a subtle flavour
while filling the kitchen with a
nose-twitching aroma. The last-
minute glaze adds a deep, rich
colour to this slow-cooked, tender
and succulent leg, which, although
it is served like a roast, is actually
braised, as it is not cooked on a
rack. Remove most of the fat to
avoid making a greasy gravy.*

1 x 2 kg (4½ lb) leg of lamb
3 cloves garlic, slivered
5 ml (1 tsp) salt and a little
 milled black pepper
10 ml (2 tsp) ground coriander
6 fairly large sprigs rosemary
250 ml (8 fl oz) hot beef stock
1 large onion, finely chopped
a little chopped parsley

GLAZE
15 ml (1 tbsp) light brown
 sugar
15 ml (1 tbsp) smooth
 apricot jam
10 ml (2 tsp) Worcestershire
 sauce
15 ml (1 tbsp) lemon juice
2.5 ml (½ tsp) curry powder

Remove thin outer membrane
and excess fat from lamb, then
wipe leg with vinegar-water.
Using a sharp knife, jab holes
here and there and insert garlic
slivers. Mix salt, pepper and
coriander, rub over leg and, if
time allows, stand for 2–3 hours.

To roast, place lamb in a roasting tin (without rack). Brush top
with oil, and place 3 rosemary
sprigs under joint and remaining
3 on top. Roast at 160 ˚C (325 ˚F,
gas 3) for 1 hour.

Pour off any fat in the roasting
tin and remove the rosemary
from the bottom. Add stock, the
onion and parsley, and return to
oven for 1¼ hours.

Mix ingredients for glaze, stirring until smooth. Remove
remaining rosemary sprigs from
lamb, add a few needles to meat
juices and discard remainder.
Brush top of joint with half the
glaze and add a little extra stock
or water to roasting tin. Return
to oven for 15 minutes. Brush
with remaining glaze and roast
for a further 15 minutes.

Transfer lamb to a serving dish
and rest in warming drawer.
Make a gravy by pouring meat
juices into a small saucepan and
thickening with a little slaked
cornflour.
Serves 6.

LAMB AND AUBERGINE CURRY

This slow-baked casserole combines tender cubes of lamb and aubergines in a thick, aromatic gravy. A good choice when entertaining as, once assembled, it bakes happily on its own without further attention. Leg or chump chops (not loin) are the best cut to use. Cheaper than buying and boning a leg, the small marrow bone in the centre of each chop adds flavour and succulence. Serve with rice (try tossing it with a nut of butter and a little toasted coconut) and the usual curry accompaniments.

575 g (1¼ lb) leg chops, trimmed of excess fat
25 ml (5 tsp) sunflower oil
1 large onion, chopped
2 cloves garlic, crushed
10 ml (2 tsp) curry powder
2.5 ml (½ tsp) turmeric
1 walnut-sized knob root ginger, peeled and grated

2.5 ml (½ tsp) each ground cinnamon, coriander and fennel
1.25 ml (¼ tsp) ground cumin
25 ml (5 tsp) flour
250 ml (8 fl oz) beef stock
250 g (9 oz) tomatoes, skinned and chopped
30 g (1 oz) seedless raisins
25 ml (5 tsp) chutney
2.5 ml (½ tsp) salt
1 bay leaf
250 g (9 oz) aubergines, cubed and dégorged (see box, page 82)
Bulgarian yoghurt

Slice each chop into three pieces. Heat oil in a large frying pan and soften onion and garlic. Add all spices and toss for 1–2 minutes over low heat to prevent scorching. Add a dash more oil and lamb, tossing until coated with spices on all sides. Sprinkle in flour, then slowly stir in stock. Add tomatoes, and when mixture starts to boil, remove from

hob and add remaining ingredients, except yoghurt. (Because aubergines are not fried before adding, it is important to dry them well so that they do not introduce extra liquid to the gravy.)

Turn into a medium-sized baking dish, cover and bake at 160 °C (325 °F, gas 3) for 1½ hours, by which time lamb should be beautifully tender and gravy richly coloured and thick.

Check seasoning, swirl a little yoghurt across top, and reheat for 5 minutes.
Serves 4.

HINT
If doubling the ingredients, use two frying pans and then combine everything in one big baking dish.

SESAME FILLET OF PORK

Soaked in an apple juice and sherry marinade, and tinged with sesame and ginger, this recipe adds character to a rather bland meat. Combined with vegetables and a gravy-like sauce, two slender fillets go quite a long way, especially if served on fried rice tossed with bean sprouts and toasted almonds.

400 g (14 oz) pork fillets, well trimmed
25 ml (5 tsp) soy sauce
5 ml (1 tsp) dark sesame oil
25 ml (5 tsp) medium-dry sherry
1 walnut-sized knob root ginger, peeled and grated or finely chopped
1 clove garlic, crushed
125 ml (4 fl oz) unsweetened apple juice
25 ml (5 tsp) sunflower oil
125 g (4 oz) white mushrooms, wiped and thinly sliced

1 medium onion, chopped
1 large red pepper, cored,
    seeded and julienned
45 ml (3 tbsp) toasted sesame
    seeds
250 ml (8 fl oz) chicken stock
10 ml (2 tsp) cornflour
extra soy sauce to taste

Butterfly fillets by making a deep
lengthwise incision along one
side and opening out. Slice
across the grain into thin strips.
Mix together soy sauce, sesame
oil, sherry, ginger, garlic and
apple juice. Place pork in a glass
dish and pour the marinade
over, mixing well, then marinate
for 1 hour. Remove pork from
the marinade and pat dry, reserving the marinade.

Heat oil in a large frying pan,
add pork and stir-fry over medium heat until tender. Remove
pork and add mushrooms, onion
and red pepper to pan. Stir-fry
until juices have evaporated.
Return pork to pan, together
with sesame seeds. Mix reserved

marinade with stock and cornflour and add to pan.

Cover and simmer very gently
for about 10 minutes, until gravy
is thick and pork cooked
through. Extra soy sauce to taste
can be added.
Serves 4.

ORANGE PORK
CHOPS

*Pork is a meat that takes really
kindly to flavoursome sauces and
the following recipe admirably
proves the point. First soaked in a
marinade based on orange juice, the
chops are slow-baked until tender.
The juices, reduced to a toffee-
coloured sauce, are poured over
each chop. The result is a seductive
harmony of flavours. Serve with
baked potatoes and soured cream,
and lightly cooked, brightly
coloured vegetables such as Brussels
sprouts and carrots.*

8 pork rib chops (about 1 kg
    (2¼ lb)), without rind and
    trimmed of excess fat*
10 ml (2 tsp) sunflower oil
125 ml (4 fl oz) fresh orange
    juice
10 ml (2 tsp) curry powder
20 ml (4 tsp) soy sauce
45 ml (3 tbsp) mild chutney
2.5 ml (½ tsp) ground
    cinnamon
10 ml (2 tsp) pale, thin honey
2.5 ml (½ tsp) very finely
    grated orange rind

Arrange chops in a single layer
in a glass or porcelain baking
dish, without overlapping. Mix
remaining ingredients and pour
over. Marinate for 1–2 hours,
turning at least twice. Cover and
bake at 160 °C (325 °F, gas 3) for
50–60 minutes. Turn and bake,
uncovered, for 15–20 minutes or
until chops are tender, and juices
still generous in quantity. (Exact
time will depend on the thickness of chops, size of dish, and
position in oven.)

Transfer chops to serving platter and keep warm. To concentrate flavour of the juices, and to
reduce slightly, pour into a small
saucepan and boil over high heat
until syrupy and light caramel in
colour – this takes only a few
minutes, and you should be careful not to boil beyond this stage.
Pour over chops – there should
be at least 25 ml (5 tsp) per chop
– and serve.
Serves 6–8.

* Rib chops look rather like
long, thick steaks with a small
L-shaped bone at one end.

PORK CHOPS AROMATIQUE

Although this dish is adapted from an Italian recipe with a very long name, it is quite one of the easiest ways of treating pork chops – simply rubbed with herbs, simmered in stock, browned in the reduced juices and finished off with a dash of wine. Minimal ingredients, maximum flavour, and much enjoyed by those who do not like their meat swathed in sauces. Good with buttered cabbage, mashed potatoes and carrots cooked in orange juice.

4 pork loin chops (about 675 g
  (1 1/2 lb))
2.5 ml (1/2 tsp) each dried
  oregano and basil, crushed
2.5 ml (1/2 tsp) salt
about 125 ml (4 fl oz) chicken
  stock
125 ml (4 fl oz) red wine or
  apple juice, or half of each
25 ml (5 tsp) cultured soured
  cream (optional)

Remove rind and some of fat from chops. Mix dried herbs with salt, rub into both sides of chops, and leave for 1 hour. Arrange chops in a single layer in a frying pan, and add stock to half the depth of chops – the exact amount of stock depends on size of pan. Bring to the boil, then cover and simmer very, very gently for 1 hour, or until tender. (Rapid boiling will result in dry, tough, chops.) If liquid has not evaporated by the time chops are tender, remove lid and cook until chops begin to brown, turning a few times.

Transfer chops to warmed serving dish. Add wine and/or juice to the pan, together with soured cream, if using. Boil, stirring, until syrupy, then spoon over chops before serving.
Makes 4 small servings.

HINT
If doubling up the ingredients, use two frying pans.

CASSEROLED PORK CHOPS WITH APPLE, SAGE AND MUSHROOMS

The flavours in this dish mingle quite marvellously and the result is one of the most enticing ways of serving pork chops. Once assembled, the chops are left to bake slowly in the oven, needing no further attention but for the addition of the fresh sage, which is stirred in towards the end of the baking time out of respect for its delicate aroma.

20 ml (4 tsp) sunflower oil
nut of butter
4-6 pork rib chops, trimmed of
  excess fat (750 g (1 3/4 lb))
1 large onion, finely chopped
250 g (9 oz) brown
  mushrooms, wiped and
  thinly sliced
1–2 cloves garlic, crushed
5 ml (1 tsp) finely grated
  lemon rind
30 ml (2 tbsp) flour
250 ml (8 fl oz) unsweetened
  apple juice
25 ml (5 tsp) soy sauce
5 ml (1 tsp) honey
12 fresh sage leaves, finely
  chopped

Heat oil and butter in a large frying pan. Add chops and brown lightly on both sides, keeping heat low in order to release any excess fat. Arrange chops in a single layer in a baking dish. Soften onion in same pan – add extra oil if necessary. Add mushrooms, garlic and lemon rind, and when softening sprinkle in flour. Slowly stir in apple juice, and when thickened add soy sauce and honey. Pour over chops. Cover; bake at 160 °C (325 °F, gas 3) for 50 minutes. Remove from oven, stir in sage and turn chops. Bake, uncovered, for a further 20–30 minutes, until chops are tender and sauce is reduced.
Serves 4.

CASEROLE OF VENISON

First soaked in a marinade of red wine and spices, then cubed and slowly simmered with bacon and vegetables, this is a delicious departure from roast venison. Serve as a fork supper on a chilly night, and surround with traditional accompaniments: Yellow Rice (see box, page 41), pumpkin baked with honey, plain green peas and a bowl of quince jelly.

3 kg (6¹/₂ lb) venison (either one large leg, or a leg and a shoulder)
25 ml (5 tsp) sunflower oil
30 g (1 oz) butter
250 g (9 oz) bacon, diced
2 large onions, chopped
2 cloves garlic, crushed
3 carrots, diced
45 ml (3 tbsp) flour
375 ml (13 fl oz) reserved marinade
375 ml (13 fl oz) stock
7.5 ml (1¹/₂ tsp) salt
7.5 ml (1¹/₂ tsp) mixed dried herbs
rind of 1 small orange, cut into large strips*
15 g (¹/₂ oz) chopped parsley
10 ml (2 tsp) brown sugar

MARINADE
750 ml (1¹/₄ pints) red wine (such as claret)
100 ml (3¹/₂ fl oz) brown vinegar
100 ml (3¹/₂ fl oz) water
8 juniper and 6 allspice berries, bruised in a mortar
8 black peppercorns
3 bay leaves
2 onions, sliced
6 whole cloves

Remove outer membrane from venison and place in a very large glass or porcelain dish suitable for marinating. Do not use a metal dish. Mix all marinade ingredients and pour over venison. Refrigerate for 48 hours, turning at least twice a day.

Remove venison, strain marinade and set aside.

Cut venison flesh from bones and use bones and trimmings to make a stock by covering them with water, adding a pinch of salt, 1 onion stuck with 2 cloves, 1 whole carrot, a dash of brown vinegar (addition of an acid ingredient helps to extract calcium from bones) and a little parsley. Strain stock and reserve.

Slice venison into small cubes, and pat dry. You should have 1.6 kg (3¹/₂ lb) cubed venison.

Heat oil and butter in a large frying pan and fry bacon and onions until lightly browned. Transfer to a large, deep baking dish, measuring about 28 x 23 x 7.5 cm (11 x 9 x 3 in). Add cubed venison to pan in batches to avoid stewing, and fry lightly, adding extra oil if necessary. Remove with a slotted spoon and add to dish with bacon and onions. Add a little more oil to pan if necessary and sauté garlic and carrots. Sprinkle in flour,

then stir in reserved marinade and stock, salt, mixed herbs, orange rind, parsley and sugar. Bring to the boil, stirring, then pour into baking dish, mixing all ingredients well.

Cover and bake at 160 °C (325 °F, gas 3) for 1 hour. Remove from oven and stir to mix. Return to oven, uncovered, and bake until meat is tender and gravy nice and thick, about 45 minutes more. If gravy is still not thick enough, stir in a little cornflour mixed with sweet sherry, and return to oven for a further 15 minutes.

Remove orange rind, check seasoning, and turn into a warmed serving dish, as baking dish will probably be too spattered to present to guests.
Serves 8.

* When using orange rind in a dish be sure to remove any white pith which could impart a bitter flavour.

BROCCOLI WITH ALMONDS AND RED PEPPER

One of the simplest, most colourful and best ways of treating this popular vegetable.

**450 g (1 lb) broccoli
a little chicken stock
salt and milled black pepper
15 ml (1 tbsp) sunflower oil
15 g (1/2 oz) butter
1 large red pepper, cored, seeded and thinly julienned
blanched, halved almonds***
dash of lemon juice

Trim tips off broccoli stems and discard. Chop stems coarsely, reserving florets. Boil stems for 10 minutes in a little chicken stock, then add florets and simmer, half-covered, until just tender. Drain if necessary, season and keep warm in a serving dish.

Heat oil and butter in a small frying pan, add red pepper and as many almonds as you wish – the more the better. When red pepper is tender-crisp and almonds lightly browned, add a dash of lemon juice, pour over broccoli and serve.
Serves 4.

* Whenever halved almonds are called for, slivered almonds may be substituted. They are sold ready-blanched, and are slightly more economical to use.

HONEYED BUTTER-NUT WITH SESAME AND GINGER

Butternuts are the most versatile of squashes. They may be sliced and baked with butter and spices, like pumpkin, or halved and stuffed before baking. The following recipe, which is easily doubled, is a delicious alternative to serve with roast lamb or chicken.

**500 g (18 oz) peeled, cubed butternut squash
25 ml (5 tsp) hulled sesame seeds
30 g (1 oz) butter, or half sunflower oil and half butter
15 ml (1 tbsp) pale, thin honey
5 ml (1 tsp) ground ginger**

Poach butternut squash in a little salted water until just tender. Drain if necessary. Place sesame seeds in a frying pan and heat gently until toasted. Add butter or butter and oil, honey and ginger, and stir until hot and melted. Add butternut squash, toss gently to mix without breaking up cubes, then cover pan and heat through gently.
Serves 4.

HINT
Pale, thin honey is used in all recipes. Dark honey often has a strong flavour, and thick honey can make a dish too sweet.

JACKET-ROASTED POTATOES

Nice and easy and much healthier than ordinary roast potatoes.

**4 medium to large potatoes, scrubbed and halved lengthwise
a little sunflower oil
salt and paprika
a few sprigs of rosemary**

Cover base of a Swiss roll tin, or a large layer cake tin, with a very thin layer of oil and heat briefly. Place potatoes in oil and turn to coat, arranging them cut-sides down. Season tops with salt and paprika, and tuck in a sprig of rosemary here and there.

Bake at any temperature from 160 °C (325 °F, gas 3) to 200 °C (400 °F, gas 6), depending on what meat you are roasting, until cooked.
Serves 8.

POTATO, MUSHROOM AND LEEK CASSEROLE

A mélange of layered vegetables, baked in stock, spiked with herb butter and topped with cheese, this dish makes an excellent accompaniment to a vegetarian meal, or serve with a simple main course such as grilled chicken or fish.

750 g (1³/₄ lb) potatoes
lemon juice
45–60 g (1¹/₂ – 2 oz) soft butter
2–3 cloves garlic, crushed
5 ml (1 tsp) finely chopped fresh rosemary needles
250 g (9 oz) white mushrooms, wiped and thinly sliced
4 large leeks, thinly sliced
salt and milled black pepper
250 ml (8 fl oz) chicken stock
grated low-fat cheese, or thinly sliced mozzarella

Peel potatoes and slice into thin rounds, dropping them into a bowl of water to which a dash of lemon juice has been added. Drain well just before using.

Mash butter with garlic and rosemary. Rub base of 30 x 20 cm (12 x 8 in) baking dish with half butter mixture, and cover with half potato slices. Top with half mushrooms and half leeks, and season. Repeat, starting with remaining mushrooms, then leeks, and finally potatoes.

Dot with remaining butter mixture. Season again and pour in stock. (Although the quantity of stock is small the mushrooms will add their juices.)

Cover securely and bake at 180 °C (350 °F, gas 4) for 50 minutes, or until potatoes are soft and most of liquid is absorbed. Sprinkle with cheese and bake, uncovered, for about 15 minutes, until cheese has melted. If liked, grill briefly until browned.
Serves 6–8.

BAKED LEMON RICE

Rice baked in the oven is convenient and fuss-free. The following makes a fine accompaniment to seafood, chicken or veal.

25 ml (5 tsp) sunflower oil
1 bunch of slender spring onions, chopped
1 large stick celery plus some leaves, chopped
5 ml (1 tsp) peeled, grated root ginger
200 g (7 oz) long-grain white rice
500 ml (17 fl oz) chicken stock
25 ml (5 tsp) soy sauce
5 ml (1 tsp) finely grated lemon rind
45 ml (3 tbsp) sherry
60 g (2 oz) toasted, slivered almonds
a nut of butter (optional)
chopped parsley for garnish

Heat oil and lightly fry onions, celery and ginger. Turn off heat and add rice, stock, soy sauce, lemon rind, sherry and almonds. Stir to mix, then tip into a 23 cm (9 in) buttered pie baking dish. Cover and bake at 160 °C (325 °F, gas 3) for 50 minutes, or until rice is cooked and liquid absorbed. Toss with a fork, adding a nut of butter, if liked, and sprinkle with parsley.
Serves 6.

GINGERED GREEN BEANS WITH WATER CHESTNUTS

Use the slimmest young green beans you can find to make this crunchy vegetable dish, the perfect companion to roast pork.

30 ml (2 tbsp) sunflower oil, or 20 ml (4 tsp) sunflower oil and 10 ml (2 tsp) dark sesame oil
2 large leeks, thinly sliced
2 cloves garlic, crushed
1 walnut-sized knob root ginger, peeled and grated
500 g (18 oz) green beans, trimmed and halved
125 ml (4 fl oz) water or vegetable stock
225 g (8 oz) canned water chestnuts, drained and sliced
25 ml (5 tsp) sweet sherry
25 ml (5 tsp) soy sauce
toasted sesame seeds to garnish

Heat oil in a large frying pan with a lid, and sauté leeks, garlic and ginger. Add beans and toss to mix. Add water or stock, then cover and boil rapidly until beans are just tender and water is absorbed. Reduce heat and add water chestnuts, sherry and soy sauce, and toss until heated through. Check seasoning. Turn into a heated serving dish, sprinkle with sesame seeds, and serve immediately.
Serves 6–8.

ROOT GINGER
The following is a convenient way of storing root ginger: peel and cut into walnut-sized knobs. Place in a glass jar and cover with sherry. Close and store in refrigerator.

APPLEY CARROTS

Really tiny carrots, simply cooked in apple juice with a whiff of cinnamon and a touch of honey, are super served with pork.

500 g (18 oz) young carrots
250 ml (8 fl oz) unsweetened apple juice
1.25 ml (¼ tsp) ground cinnamon
100 ml (7 tbsp) finely chopped parsley
2.5 ml (½ tsp) salt
10 ml (2 tsp) pale, thin honey

Place carrots in a large, shallow saucepan. Pour apple juice over, dust with cinnamon, sprinkle with parsley and salt, then drizzle over honey. Bring to the boil, then reduce heat and simmer gently, covered, for 30–40 minutes, or until carrots are crisp-tender and liquid has almost boiled away.
Serves 8–10.

TO REGULATE HEAT
In almost every recipe it is vital to be able to reduce cooking heat quickly. Many a dish has been ruined by boiling when a slow simmer is required. If using gas, regulating the heat is more or less instant, and a stove fitted with spiral plates is also quite quick to obey. If, however, you have a stove with solid plates, you might have to remove the saucepan while the plate cools down. Otherwise, place one of those round, metal perforated discs, which are specially designed for this, under the saucepan when a sudden slow-simmer is required. Do not use an asbestos mat.

PATTY PAN SQUASH AU GRATIN

Tiny patty pans are closely related to custard squash, but somewhat younger. Because of their delicate flavour, they are at their best served simply steamed. Then again, when covered with a mustard sauce and melting cheese, they become a talked-about accompaniment to grilled chicken, fish or steak. Perfect for entertaining, as the entire dish may be assembled in advance – with another plus – an instantly mixed coating sauce, using a blender. This dish also makes a super vegetarian meal served with brown rice tossed with lentils and fried mushrooms doused in soy sauce.

500 ml (17 fl oz) chicken stock
a little chopped onion
1 bouquet garni
575 g (1 ¼ lb) patty pan squash (about 28), preferably yellow and green

SAUCE
250 ml (8 fl oz) reserved poaching liquid
250 ml (8 fl oz) milk
60 ml (4 tbsp) flour
1.25 ml (¼ tsp) salt
25 ml (5 tsp) sunflower oil
30 g (1 oz) butter
5 ml (1 tsp) mustard powder
10–15 ml (2–3 tsp) wholegrain mustard
a squeeze of lemon juice
125–150 g (4–5 oz) finely grated cheese, such as medium-fat Edam

In a saucepan large enough to take patty pans in a single layer, bring stock, onion and bouquet garni to the boil. Add patty pans and cook, covered, for about 10 minutes, or until easily pierced with tip of a sharp knife. Strain poaching liquid and reserve. Using a slotted spoon, arrange patty pans in a single layer in a lightly oiled baking dish. They should cover base fairly snugly. If necessary, slice off points.

To make sauce, put poaching liquid, milk, flour, salt, oil, butter and mustard powder in a blender goblet and blend well. Pour into heavy-based saucepan rinsed with water to prevent scorching, and cook over low heat, stirring. When mixture thickens and becomes creamy yellow, simmer gently, uncovered, for about 5 minutes to cook flour. Remove from heat and stir in wholegrain mustard, lemon juice and, if necessary, a pinch of salt.

Pour sauce evenly over patty pans and sprinkle with cheese. (If preparing in advance, set aside at this stage, and when needed, bake in a moderate oven until hot and just beginning to bubble.) Place patty pans under grill until cheese is golden brown and melted.
Serves 4-6.

STIR-FRIED COURGETTES

Grated and stir-fried, this ultra-quick method is more of a tip than a recipe, but definitely worth noting.

45 ml (3 tbsp) sunflower oil
575 g (1 ¼ lb) small courgettes, pared and coarsely grated
a few spring onions, chopped
2 cloves garlic, crushed
125 g (4 oz) bean sprouts of choice
45 g (1 ½ oz) toasted sunflower seeds
20 ml (4 tsp) soy sauce

Heat oil in a large, shallow saucepan, add courgettes, spring onions and garlic. Stir-fry for about 1 minute – the marrows must still be crisp, not wilted. Add bean sprouts, sunflower seeds and soy sauce, tossing to mix. Heat through and serve.
Serves 6–8.

BRUSSELS SPROUTS WITH MUSTARD, HONEY AND NUTMEG

These delicately flavoured, minuscule cabbages are best served very simply – steamed and then tossed with a little butter and lemon juice – but when served on a special occasion, as with the Christmas turkey, they respond well to a little extra attention.

500 g (18 oz) Brussels sprouts
250 ml (8 fl oz) chicken stock or salted water*
1.25 ml (¼ tsp) freshly grated nutmeg
10 ml (2 tsp) pale, thin honey
20 ml (4 tsp) fresh lemon juice
20 g (¾ oz) butter
5 ml (1 tsp) Dijon mustard (or more to taste)

Remove outer leaves from sprouts, nick a cross in stem end of each, and rinse well. Using a large, shallow saucepan, bring stock or salted water, nutmeg and honey to the boil. Add sprouts, cover, and cook briefly, until just tender. Drain if necessary. Add lemon juice, butter and mustard, and toss to mix. Serve when butter has melted.
Serves 6–8.

* If using frozen Brussels sprouts, use only 125 ml (4 fl oz) lightly seasoned chicken stock or water.

GOURMET STIR-FRIED VEGETABLES

I do not usually combine vegetables when serving them as an accompaniment to a main course, because I believe that if perfectly cooked, they should stand alone to be appreciated. The following recipe, however, is an exception. This crisp, flavoursome medley which includes mangetout - one of today's nouvelle vegetables – goes beautifully with roast meats, grilled fish, or chicken, and is cooked in a matter of minutes. If preferred, it may also be served as a crunchy salad – simply cool, cover and chill until required.

30 ml (2 tbsp) sunflower oil*
1 large bunch of spring onions, chopped
1–2 cloves garlic, crushed
250 g (9 oz) courgettes, pared and very thinly julienned
250 g (9 oz) white mushrooms, wiped and sliced
150 g (5 oz) mangetout, topped and tailed
30 g (1 oz) shredded spinach leaves
25 ml (5 tsp) each soy sauce and water
pinch of sugar
toasted sesame seeds or slivered almonds for garnish

Heat oil in a large frying pan, add spring onions, garlic and courgettes, and toss over low heat until just beginning to wilt. Add remaining ingredients, and cook, tossing, for 2–3 minutes, until tender-crisp. Spoon into a warmed serving dish and top with garnish.
Serves 4.

* Sesame oil may be substituted for part of the sunflower oil. Remember that light sesame oil is much milder in flavour than the dark variety – in the case of the latter, use only 5–10 ml (1–2 tsp).

VARIATION
For a vegetarian meal, garnish very generously with the seeds or nuts, and serve on a bed of cooked brown rice and lentils moistened with a nut of butter.

ORANGE RICE

This perfumed rice is perfect with pork or chicken, and may be cooked on the hob or baked in the oven.

200 g (7 oz) long-grain white
  or brown rice
500 ml (17 fl oz) water or
  lightly seasoned chicken
  stock (plus 45 ml (3 tbsp)
  extra if using brown rice)
10 ml (2 tsp) finely grated
  orange rind
30 g (1 oz) seedless raisins
2.5 ml (½ tsp) salt
10 ml (2 tsp) sunflower oil
2 sticks cinnamon

Place all ingredients in a heavy-based saucepan, stir once to mix, using a fork, then bring to the boil. Cover and simmer until liquid is absorbed – about 25 minutes for white rice, 50 minutes for brown. Alternatively, place all ingredients in a baking dish, cover and bake, increasing time if using brown rice.
Serves 4–6.

PATTY PAN SQUASH WITH LEMON AND GARLIC BUTTER

In this recipe, cooked patty pans are simply tossed in fragrant butter, with walnut oil adding a gourmet touch. The oil also prevents the butter from browning, and means that the dish may be prepared in advance and heated through at dinner time. This is really just a basic recipe to illustrate how easy it is to add a little zing to the flavour of any delicate vegetable.

12 small, yellow patty pan
  squashes
15 g (½ oz) butter
15 ml (1 tbsp) walnut oil
2.5 ml (½ tsp) finely grated
  lemon rind
1 small clove garlic, crushed

Cook patty pans in a little salted water until just tender. Drain if necessary. Heat remaining ingredients in a small frying pan or flameproof serving dish. Add patty pans in a single layer and heat through gently. Spoon buttery juices over each serving.
Serves 4.

GRILLED MEDITERRANEAN VEGETABLES

Grilled vegetables – richly browned, crisp and juicy – have become very fashionable. Grouped or piled on a platter, they make a colourful display and are absolutely delicious with grilled meats. They may also be served cold as a salad, and will keep for up to two days if refrigerated. To avoid last-minute grilling and basting, I have devised the following recipe in which the vegetables are left to marinate in a garlicky dressing and then grilled just before dinner. This innovative method is not as straightforward as boiling or steaming, but well worth the extra effort.

1 medium aubergine (about
  300 g (11 oz))
10 yellow patty pan squashes
  (about 350 g (12 oz)), or 350 g
  (12 oz) courgettes
250 g (9 oz) medium-sized
  white mushrooms, wiped
3 large peppers (one red, one
  yellow and one green), cored,
  seeded and julienned
150 g (5 oz) slim young carrots,
  halved lengthwise
salt and milled black pepper
large pinch of sugar
25 ml (5 tsp) olive oil

MARINADE
75 ml (5 tbsp) olive oil
75 ml (5 tbsp) sunflower oil
7.5 ml (1¹/₂ tsp) dried
  origanum
3 cloves garlic, crushed
1.25 ml (¹/₄ tsp) dried thyme

Wash aubergine, slice off stalk end, cut in half through the middle, vertically, slice into long fingers, like chips, and dégorge (see box, alongside). Nick off tops and bottoms from patty pans, and then slice each across into three rings; if using courgettes, pare and slice into thick finger lengths. Mix all vegetables in a large porcelain dish. Mix ingredients for marinade, pour over vegetables and toss until well mixed and glistening. Cover and leave vegetables to marinate for about 2 hours, tossing occasionally.

Just before grilling, season vegetables with salt, pepper and sugar. Preheat grill. Place vegetables on rack in 40 x 30 cm (16 x 12 in) roasting tin – a meat roasting tin, complete with fitted rack, is ideal. Position roasting tin as far below grill as possible. The vegetables will slowly start to soften, bubble and brown, and will be ready in about 13 minutes. Return vegetables to porcelain baking dish, drizzle the top with olive oil, and place in moderately hot oven for a few minutes to heat through thoroughly. (If you are serving pittas as an accompaniment to the meal, heat them at the same time.)
Serves 6 as an accompaniment, and 4 as a main course.

HINT
If you're having to feed a crowd, don't attempt to pile the increased quantity of vegetables onto the rack in too thick a layer. Rather do them in two batches, keeping the first batch warm in the warming drawer while grilling the second.

DÉGORGING BRINJALS
This is a process which extracts the bitter juices. Wash aubergines, slice or cube them, place in colander, salt quite heavily, and put weight on top. Leave for 30–45 minutes, then rinse and dry well. Rinsing and drying the aubergines is important, to avoid adding excess salt and liquid to the dish. Use either a salad spinner or paper towels.

MUSHROOM RICE

A popular old favourite, at home with almost anything.

45 ml (3 tbsp) sunflower oil
1 bunch of spring onions, chopped
1 green or red pepper, cored, seeded and diced
1 large stick celery, thinly sliced
250 g (9 oz) brown mushrooms, wiped and thinly sliced
5 ml (1 tsp) chopped fresh rosemary needles
45 ml (3 tbsp) sweet sherry
400 g (13 oz) cooked white or brown rice
25 ml (5 tsp) soy sauce
toasted, chopped almonds (optional)

Heat oil and sauté onions, pepper and celery. Reduce heat, add mushrooms and rosemary, and toss until mushrooms start to shrink. Add sherry and allow to bubble briefly. Add rice, soy sauce and almonds, if using. Using a fork, toss lightly, until well mixed and heated through. Serves 6–8.

BAKED PINEAPPLE RICE

Perfect with turkey, or pork.

45 ml (3 tbsp) sunflower oil
1 onion, finely chopped
1 red pepper or half a red and half a green pepper, cored, seeded and diced
2 slices fresh pineapple, cored and finely diced
175 g (6 oz) long-grain white rice
400 ml (14 fl oz) hot water
45 ml (3 tbsp) chopped parsley
5 ml (1 tsp) salt
30 g (1 oz) seedless raisins
a nut of butter (optional)

Heat oil in a frying pan and soften onion, peppers and pineapple. Add rice; toss with a fork until mixed. Mix in remaining ingredients, except butter; turn into a deep, 20 cm (8 in) pie baking dish. (If preparing in advance, set aside at this stage.)

Bake, covered, at 160 °C (325 °F, gas 3) for about 45 minutes, or until liquid is absorbed and rice is cooked. Do not stir while baking. Just before serving, toss with a fork to mix, adding a nut of butter, if liked.
Serves 4–6.

GREEN BEANS WITH FRESH HERB BUTTER

Ripe with the aroma of fresh herbs and crunchy with sunflower seeds, these beans are astonishingly good. Serve hot, or cold as a salad.

30 g (1 oz) butter, or half butter and half sunflower oil
1 small clove garlic, crushed
1 sprig each of thyme and marjoram, leaves chopped
4–6 sage leaves, chopped
400 g (14 oz) young green beans, trimmed and halved
2 leeks, thinly sliced
salt and milled black pepper
45 ml (3 tbsp) sunflower seeds

Cream butter or butter and oil with garlic and herbs, and set aside. Poach beans and leeks in a little water until just tender, then drain if necessary. Return to saucepan, season, add creamed butter, and stir over low heat until melted and fragrant. Toss in sunflower seeds and serve immediately.
Serves 6–8.

VARIATION
To serve as a salad, it is essential to use half butter and half oil.

NUTTY BARLEY PILAFF WITH SPICES

Pearl barley is a delicious, wholesome grain. It is an important ingredient in Scotch Broth, but really deserves wider recognition. It may simply be boiled and served instead of rice, or as follows.

25 ml (5 tsp) sunflower oil
a nut of butter
1 bunch of spring onions, chopped
1 stick cinnamon
4 whole cloves
2.5 ml (1/2 tsp) turmeric
5 ml (1 tsp) ground coriander
200 g (7 oz) pearl barley, rinsed and drained*
600 ml (1 pint) chicken stock
2.5 ml (1/2 tsp) salt
30 g (1 oz) seedless raisins
60 ml (4 tbsp) chopped, toasted macadamia nuts or sunflower seeds

Heat oil and butter in a heavy, wide-based saucepan. Add spring onions and spices and toss over low heat until sizzling. Add barley, 250 ml (8 fl oz) of stock and salt. Stir through with a fork, then cover and simmer for 15 minutes. (Keep heat very low throughout the cooking period or barley will catch on the bottom of the saucepan.) Add remaining stock and raisins, and simmer, covered, for a further 45 minutes, or a little longer, to ensure barley is tender and liquid absorbed. Turn off heat, cover saucepan with a tea-towel, and stand for 10 minutes. Fork in macadamia nuts or sunflower seeds just before serving.
Serves 4–5.

* Pearl barley, which has been husked and polished, is the one to use, as opposed to wholegrain or pot barley, which requires longer cooking periods.

MINTY BULGUR PILAFF

Although bulgur is most often enjoyed cold, as a salad, it may also be cooked and served as a delicious alternative to rice.

25 ml (5 tsp) sunflower oil
180 g (6 oz) bulgur*
1 onion, thinly sliced into rings
1 clove garlic, crushed
2.5–5 ml (1/2–1 tsp) salt
500 ml (17 fl oz) chicken stock
100 ml (7 tbsp) chopped parsley
about 20 ml (4 tsp) finely chopped fresh mint leaves
a nut of butter

Heat oil in a large frying pan, add bulgur, onion and garlic, and toss for a few minutes over low heat. Add salt, stock and parsley, stir to mix, bring to the boil, then cover and cook very gently for about 15 minutes, or until water is absorbed. (If preparing in advance, set aside at this stage. Reheat over low heat, adding a little extra stock or water to pan.) Fork in mint and butter just before serving.
Serves 6.

* Use the pre-cooked variety, available from wholefood shops and some supermarkets.

VARIATION
For a Mushroom Pilaff, add diced mushrooms when frying bulgur and onion, and omit the mint.

BAKED BUTTERNUT SQUASH WITH ORANGE JUICE AND CINNAMON

So simple, this recipe will act as more of a reminder than an inspiration. It is in keeping with today's trend towards serving less rich accompaniments with meat. It teams up beautifully with roast lamb, and can be conveniently baked in the oven at the same time.

750 g (1³/₄ lb) butternut squash
2.5 ml (¹/₂ tsp) salt
1.25 ml (¹/₄ tsp) paprika
30 ml (2 tbsp) soft brown sugar
1.25–2.5 ml (¹/₄–¹/₂ tsp) ground cinnamon
about 175 ml (6 fl oz) fresh orange juice

Peel butternut squash, slice into rings, discard pips, and cut into medium-sized cubes or triangles.

Arrange in a single layer in a large, shallow, well-buttered baking dish. Sprinkle with salt, paprika, sugar and cinnamon, then pour orange juice around sides. Cover and bake at 160 °C (325 °F, gas 3) for about 1 hour. If butternut squash is not soft and orange juice has not been absorbed, uncover and return to oven for a short while. If juice has evaporated and squash is still too firm, add a little more juice and bake until done.
Serves 4–6.

SPICED SAFFRON RICE

A fragrant, lemon-coloured rice which gives a lift to any curry or Eastern dish. The ingredients are interchangeable – turmeric may be used instead of saffron, and Basmati rice instead of regular long-grain.

25 ml (5 tsp) sunflower oil, or 20 ml (4 tsp) oil and a nut of butter
1 medium onion, finely chopped
2.5 ml (¹/₂ tsp) cumin seeds
5 ml (1 tsp) ground coriander
4 whole cloves
4 cardamom pods, bruised
1 stick cinnamon
200 g (7 oz) long-grain white or Basmati rice*
2.5 ml (¹/₂ tsp) salt
500 ml (17 fl oz) water or chicken stock
pinch of saffron threads soaked in 25 ml (5 tsp) hot water, or 2.5 ml (¹/₂ tsp) turmeric mixed with 25 ml (5 tsp) water**
100 ml (7 tbsp) chopped parsley

Heat oil or oil and butter, add onion, and soften without browning. Add all spices, except saffron or turmeric, and toss over low heat for about 2 minutes. Add rice and toss to coat, then add remaining ingredients, except parsley. Cover; cook gently over low heat for about 25 minutes, until liquid is absorbed. Remove cinnamon stick, cloves and cardamom pods. (If preparing early, cover saucepan with a tea-towel and lid; set aside. When reheating, add a dash of water or stock to mixture.) Fork in parsley just before serving.
Serves 5–6.

* If using Basmati rice, wash very well, discard any bits that float to top, and soak for 30 minutes. Drain before using. Use 750 ml (1¹/₄ pints) water or stock, simmer for about 20 minutes, and leave for 10 minutes before serving, or steam in a colander.

** Saffron is frequently used in Indian cooking. Because it is so expensive, turmeric may be substituted. If using saffron, soak the threads in a little warm water for up to 1¹/₂ hours before using, to release the colour and flavour.

SEAFOOD PASTA

A great choice for an informal fork supper as it is easily doubled to feed a crowd, and may be completely assembled in advance.

375–400 g (13–14 oz) skinned
  fish fillets (frozen whiting is
  perfectly suitable)
225 g (8 oz) canned mussels in
  brine, drained and roughly
  chopped
200 g (7 oz) medium ribbon
  noodles, cooked and well
  drained
100 ml (3¹/₂ fl oz) reserved fish
  stock
25 ml (5 tsp) grated Parmesan
  cheese
paprika

TOMATO SAUCE
15 ml (1 tbsp) sunflower oil
1 large onion, chopped
2 cloves garlic, crushed
2.5 ml (¹/₂ tsp) dried oregano
2.5 ml (¹/₂ tsp) dried basil

400 g (14 oz) canned tomatoes,
  chopped, plus the juice
15 ml (1 tbsp) tomato purée
2 bay leaves
2.5 ml (¹/₂ tsp) salt
5 ml (1 tsp) sugar
45 ml (3 tbsp) red wine

CHEESE SAUCE
25 ml (5 tsp) sunflower oil
30 g (1 oz) butter
60 ml (4 tbsp) flour
250 ml (8 fl oz) reserved fish
  stock
250 ml (8 fl oz) milk,
  preferably heated
large pinch of freshly grated
  nutmeg
salt and pepper
60 g (2 oz) finely grated
  Cheddar cheese

Poach fish in 375 ml (13 fl oz) salted water with a little lemon juice, 1 chopped onion and a little parsley. Cool fish in stock. Strain stock (you should have 350 ml (12 fl oz)) and reserve. Flake fish.

To make tomato sauce, heat oil, add onion, garlic and herbs, and soften without browning. Add remaining ingredients, cover and simmer for 20 minutes, stirring occasionally. Remove bay leaves, tip sauce into a large bowl, add flaked fish, mussels, cooked pasta and reserved fish stock (about 100 ml (3¹/₂ fl oz)).

To make cheese sauce, melt oil and butter, sprinkle in flour, and stir briefly over low heat to cook without browning. Slowly add reserved fish stock and milk, and cook, stirring, until sauce thickens, then simmer for a few minutes. This is a medium-thick, rather than thick sauce. Remove from hob and add remaining ingredients, stirring until cheese has melted.

To assemble, brush a 30 cm x 20 cm (12 x 8 in) baking dish with oil. Spoon in fish mixture in an even layer. Pour cheese sauce over to cover top. Sprinkle with Parmesan and dust with paprika. (The dish may now be set aside if made in advance, or if refrigerated, be sure to use a refrigerator-to-oven baking dish.) Bake at 180 ˚C (350 ˚F, gas 4) for about 30 minutes, until bubbly. **Serves 6.**

HINT
The ingredients for this recipe may be doubled to serve 12, in which case use two medium-sized baking dishes.

SEAFOOD, PASTA AND PESTO SALAD

This is a dish to serve when you want to impress, and are willing to take time over creating a dazzling, talked-about salad. Despite the fussy-sounding ingredients, it is not difficult to prepare and most of it is made in advance. Serve as a glamorous starter, or as the main course at an elegant summer lunch, with a green salad and a crusty loaf.

200 g (7 oz) fettucine
mussels in shells (rinsed and
drained if canned), black
olives and chopped fresh
basil for garnish

SQUID-TOMATO SAUCE
45 ml (3 tbsp) olive or
sunflower oil
2 leeks, very thinly sliced
1 red pepper, cored, seeded
and diced
400 g (14 oz) cleaned squid
tubes, washed, well dried and
cut into thin rings
400 g (14 oz) ripe tomatoes,
skinned and chopped*
15 ml (1 tbsp) tomato purée
45 ml (3 tbsp) full-bodied
red wine
2 bay leaves
2.5 ml (½ tsp) each salt and
sugar
milled black pepper
30 ml (2 tbsp) prepared pesto
(see box)

To make sauce, heat oil in a large
frying pan, add leeks and red
pepper, and soften over low
heat. Add squid and toss until
rings stiffen and turn white. Add
remaining ingredients, except
pesto, stir to mix, then cover and
simmer over very low heat – it
should barely bubble – for about
1 hour, stirring occasionally. At
end of cooking period squid
should be very tender and the
sauce plentiful, but somewhat
thickened. Transfer to a container and cool. Stir in pesto, then
refrigerate overnight.

Cook fettucine just before serving. Drain, turn into a bowl.

To assemble, mix squid-tomato
sauce with fettucine and toss,
using two forks, until well
mixed. Taste – for a stronger
flavour add up to 15 ml (1 tbsp)
pesto. Serve immediately, garnished as suggested.
**Serves 8 as a starter, and 4 as a
main dish.**

* Fresh tomatoes are vital – the
plum variety provides a really
fine flavour.

PARSLEY PESTO
*An alternative to traditional pesto
when basil is out of season.*

45 g (1 ½ oz) (about 36)
pecan halves
1 clove garlic, peeled
90 g (3 oz) parsley sprigs
45 ml (3 tbsp) loosely packed
fresh marjoram leaves
30 g (1 oz) soft butter
45 ml (3 tbsp) freshly grated
Parmesan cheese
pinch of salt
about 150 ml (¼ pint) olive
oil, or half olive and half sunflower oil

Place all ingredients, except oil,
in a food processor and process
until finely chopped. Slowly add
oil, while processing, until mixture forms a thick purée. Spoon
into a glass jar, run a thin film of
extra oil over surface, and
refrigerate.
Makes about 325 ml (11 fl oz).

PESTO
*Clever cooks make this in quantity
when fresh basil is available and
keep a supply in the freezer.*

60 g (2 oz) fresh basil leaves
20 g (¾ oz) parsley sprigs
2–3 cloves garlic, peeled
12 large walnut halves (about
60 g (2 oz))
45–75 ml (3–5 tbsp) finely
grated Parmesan cheese
about 175 ml (6 fl oz) olive oil
salt and milled black pepper

Place all ingredients, except oil
and seasoning, in a food processor fitted with grinding blade
and process until very finely
chopped. With motor still running, slowly dribble in oil in a
steady stream to make a thick,
green purée. Add seasoning,
then spoon into a jar. Run a thin
film of extra oil over top, to preserve the colour, cover and
refrigerate.

SPAGHETTI WITH CLAMS AND MUSHROOMS

A distant relative of the famous Italian dish. Because canned clams can be quite dull – and expensive – I have added mushrooms. I like to sneak in a little Parmesan cheese and a dollop of flavoured butter. The result is a jolly nice and easy variation of Spaghetti alle Vongole.

45 ml (3 tbsp) olive oil
1 large onion, chopped
3 cloves garlic, crushed
250 g (9 oz) white mushrooms, wiped and sliced
2.5 ml (¹/2 tsp) dried oregano
2.5 ml (¹/2 tsp) dried basil
500 g (18 oz) ripe, juicy tomatoes, skinned and chopped (not canned)
15 ml (1 tbsp) tomato purée
2 bay leaves
2.5 ml (¹/2 tsp) salt
5 ml (1 tsp) sugar
45 ml (3 tbsp) off-dry white wine
400 g (14 oz) canned baby clams in water, drained grated Parmesan cheese (optional)
300 g (11 oz) spaghetti garlic butter, or butter mixed with chopped fresh basil (optional)

Heat oil, add onion and garlic, and soften without browning. Add mushrooms and herbs, and toss until mushrooms start to shrink. Add tomatoes, tomato purée, bay leaves, salt, sugar and wine. Cover and simmer very gently for 15 minutes over lowest possible heat. Stir occasionally to mash tomatoes and, if mixture seems dry, add a dash of water. On other hand, if it is too juicy, tilt the lid slightly to expel excess moisture. Finished sauce should be juicy, but thick. Remove bay leaves, stir in clams, and heat through. Check seasoning, adding a little Parmesan, if using, for a flavour boost. In the meantime, boil pasta. Drain well and serve with sauce. If indulging in addition of butter, top each serving with a pat of your choice. Hand a pepper mill at the table.
Serves 4.

ROASTED VEGETABLE AND PASTA SALAD

This is a magnificent party salad: a medley of vegetables, marinated in oil with fresh herbs, baked until succulent, then tossed with pasta. It may be made up to two days ahead and left to `ripen' in the refrigerator. Serve on a platter with crusty bread, black olives, yoghurt and feta or goat's milk cheese.

500 g (18 oz) aubergines, cubed and dégorged (see box, page 82)
3 large yellow peppers (about 300 g) (11 oz)), cored, seeded and julienned
500 g (18 oz) courgettes, pared and julienned
250–300 g (9–11 oz) brown mushrooms, wiped and halved or quartered
2–4 slender leeks, sliced into 4 cm pieces
100 ml (3¹/2 fl oz) each olive and sunflower oil
3 cloves garlic, crushed
45 ml (3 tbsp) lemon juice
5 ml (1 tsp) salt
5 ml (1 tsp) sugar
4 large sprigs each fresh rosemary, thyme and marjoram
250 g (9 oz) broccoli florets
175 g (6 oz) elbow macaroni

Place aubergines, peppers, courgettes, mushrooms and leeks in a very large porcelain baking dish, measuring at least 28 cm x 23 cm x 7.5 cm (11 x 9 x 3 in). Mix oils, garlic, lemon juice, salt and sugar, and pour over. Tuck

in herbs and toss to mix. Cover and leave to stand for about 2 hours, tossing occasionally.

Bake, uncovered, at 220 °C (425 °F, gas 7) for 20 minutes. Remove from oven and toss to mix. Reduce temperature to 180 °C (350 °F, gas 4), and bake for a further 20 minutes, or until vegetables are juicy and tender. Remove stalks of herbs – most of the leaves will have fallen off, adding their flavour to juices.

Steam broccoli until just tender, then drain. Cook pasta and drain well. Mix broccoli and pasta with baked vegetables. Set aside, covered, to cool. Serve at room temperature, or refrigerate until needed.
Serves 8–10.

HINT
Fresh herbs add so much flavour to a dish that the amount of salt used can always be reduced to the absolute minimum.

PASTITSIO

A layered dish of macaroni, mince, and a creamy sauce with cheese and spices, frequently prepared on Greek holidays and for festive family meals. Serve in large squares, with a Greek salad and crusty bread. The one imperative is to use freshly grated Parmesan cheese.

250 g (9 oz) ready-cut macaroni

MEAT SAUCE
30 ml (2 tbsp) olive oil
1 large onion, chopped
2 cloves garlic, crushed
500 g (18 oz) lean minced beef
125 ml (4 fl oz) red wine
125 ml (4 fl oz) beef stock
250 ml (8 fl oz) tomato passata
100 ml (7 tbsp) chopped parsley
5 ml (1 tsp) each salt and sugar
2.5 ml (1/2 tsp) ground cinnamon

CHEESE SAUCE
30 g (1 oz) butter
30 ml (2 tbsp) sunflower oil
75 ml (5 tbsp) flour
750 ml (1 1/4 pints) hot milk
2.5 ml (1/2 tsp) each salt and freshly grated nutmeg
pinch of white pepper
2 eggs, beaten
45 g (1 1/2 oz) grated Parmesan cheese

TOPPING
45 ml (3 tbsp) freshly grated Parmesan cheese
45 ml (3 tbsp) fine, breadcrumbs
a few slivers of butter

To make meat sauce, heat oil and sauté onion and garlic. Add mince and toss until it turns brown and crumbly. Add remaining ingredients, stir to mix, then cover and simmer gently for 30 minutes, stirring occasionally. Finished sauce should be richly coloured and thickened but very moist.

Cook macaroni, drain well and toss with a dash of oil.

To make cheese sauce, heat butter and oil, stir in flour and cook until straw-coloured. Slowly add milk and stir until thickened, then add salt, nutmeg and pepper. Pour a little hot sauce onto beaten eggs, then stir back into sauce. Add cheese, and give it all a good whisk.

To assemble, brush a 28 x 23 x 7.5 cm (11 x 9 x 3 in) baking dish with oil. Cover base with half the cooked macaroni. Spread meat sauce over evenly. Pour half the cheese sauce over, top with remaining macaroni, then pour remaining cheese sauce over.

To make the topping, mix cheese and breadcrumbs and sprinkle over the cheese sauce. Dot with butter, then bake, uncovered, at 160 °C (325 °F, gas 3) for 50 minutes. Turn off oven and leave to settle for 15–20 minutes.
Makes 8 very large servings.

PASTA AND AUBERGINES ALLA PARMIGIANA

Tucking a layer of pasta into this traditional combination of vegetables and cheese transforms it into a hearty main course. An excellent alternative is to substitute chickpeas for the pasta. Either way, this recipe makes an economical Italian-style meal, with the added advantage of grilling the aubergine slices – try this method and you will never revert to relays of oily frying. Another bonus is that the entire dish may be assembled the day before and refrigerated overnight. Furthermore, quantities can easily be increased if you're planning an informal party. The best accompaniments are a simple green salad and crusty bread.

15 ml (1 tbsp) olive oil
1 medium onion, finely
  chopped
1–2 cloves garlic, crushed
2.5 ml (¹/₂ tsp) dried basil
2.5 ml (¹/₂ tsp) dried oregano
400 g (14 oz) canned tomatoes,
  chopped, plus the juice
10 ml (2 tsp) tomato purée
45 ml (3 tbsp) red wine
2.5 ml (¹/₂ tsp) salt
5 ml (1 tsp) sugar
2 bay leaves
45 ml (3 tbsp) chopped parsley
400 g (14 oz) aubergines, sliced
  into 6 mm rings, and
  dégorged (see box, page 82)
sunflower oil for grilling
100 g (3¹/₂ oz) elbow
  macaroni, cooked and
  drained, or 175 g (6 oz)
  cooked chickpeas
200 g (7 oz) mozzarella or
  other melting cheese, thinly
  sliced
25 ml (5 tsp) grated Parmesan
  cheese

Heat olive oil and briefly sauté onion, garlic and dried herbs over low heat. Add tomatoes, tomato purée, wine, salt, sugar, bay leaves and parsley, and simmer, covered, for 15–20 minutes, stirring occasionally. Sauce should be plentiful and juicy. Remove bay leaves and set aside.

Meanwhile, cover base of a 37 x 25 cm (15 x 10 in) baking tray with a thin layer of sunflower oil and heat gently under grill until just hot, not smoking. Arrange aubergine slices on tray, turning once to coat. Place tray on middle shelf of the oven and grill until aubergines are soft and juicy, turning once.

Lightly oil a deep, 20 cm (8 in) baking dish and cover base with half the prepared tomato sauce. Top with half the aubergine slices and cover with all the pasta or chickpeas. Top with half the sliced cheese. Repeat layers, and top with Parmesan. (Dish may now be cooled and refrigerated, but return to room temperature before baking.) Bake uncovered at 180 °C (350 °F, gas 4) for 30 minutes. **Serves 4.**

CHICKEN, VEGETABLE AND NOODLE BAKE

This meal-in-a-dish is definitely not haute cuisine. The sauce comes from a can, and the method of preparation will surely cause raised eyebrows – but haute useful it certainly is. The chicken can be poached while the pasta and broccoli are boiling while the mushrooms and onions are frying while you're crumbling the crumbs and grating the cheese. All this might leave you a little breathless, but the result is a super, substantial supper at speed. Serve with a tossed salad and hot garlic bread.

350–400 g (12–14 oz) skinned,
  filleted chicken breasts
1 onion quartered
250 g (9 oz) pasta screws
300 g (11 oz) broccoli florets
30 ml (2 tbsp) sunflower oil
a nut of butter

2 medium onions, finely
  chopped
250 g (9 oz) brown
  mushrooms, wiped and sliced
5 ml (1 tsp) dried tarragon,
  crushed between the fingers
2 x 425 g cans condensed
  mushroom soup
400 ml (14 fl oz) milk
30 ml (2 tbsp) medium-dry
  sherry
125 g (4 oz) fine, stale
  breadcrumbs
250 ml (3½ oz) grated cheese*
a few slivers of butter

Poach the chicken in a little salted water with onion for about
10 minutes, or until it is just
cooked. Cool, then drain and
dice chicken.
  Meanwhile, bring a large
saucepan of salted water to a
rapid boil. Add pasta and broccoli slowly, so that water does
not go off the boil. Cook, uncovered, over high heat for about 8
minutes, or until just cooked,
then drain.

Heat oil and butter and sauté
chopped onions, mushrooms
and tarragon for a few minutes.
Stir in the soup, milk and sherry.
  In a large bowl, mix together
diced chicken, pasta, broccoli
and sauce. Turn into a buttered
28 x 22 cm (11 x 9 in) baking
dish, cover and heat through at
160 °C (325 °F, gas 3) for 15 minutes. Sprinkle with breadcrumbs
mixed with cheese, and dot with
butter. Increase oven temperature to 180 °C (350 °F, gas 4),
and bake for a further 20–25
minutes, until bubbling and
cheese has melted.
Serves 8–10.

* Use any tasty cheese, with the
addition of grated Parmesan in
the ratio of about 3:1.

MUSHROOM PASTA WITH FRESH THYME AND CREAM

*Despite the simplicity of both the
ingredients and preparation, this is
not everyday pasta. Although best
served right in the kitchen, ladled
straight from the saucepan, it
requires caring diners. So seat six
gourmet friends round your kitchen
table, uncork some good red wine,
and allow yourself about 10 minutes at the cooker. Be sure not to
overcook this dish, especially after
adding the thyme, for the last-
minute contribution allows its
singular fragrance to come singing
through.*

250 g (9 oz) fusilli or pasta
  screws
30 ml (2 tbsp) olive oil
3 leeks, thinly sliced
250 g (9 oz) brown
  mushrooms, wiped and sliced
2 cloves garlic, crushed

400 g (14 oz) ripe tomatoes,
  skinned and chopped
15 ml (1 tbsp) tomato purée
5 ml (1 tsp) each salt and sugar
60 ml (4 tbsp) red wine
200 ml (7 fl oz) single cream
10 ml (2 tsp) fresh thyme
  leaves
45 ml (3 tbsp) chopped parsley
45 ml (3 tbsp) freshly grated
  Parmesan cheese

Cook pasta and drain well, tossing with a dash of oil.
  Meanwhile, heat olive oil in a
large saucepan, add leeks and
allow to soften over low heat.
Add mushrooms and garlic, and
toss until aromatic, then add
tomatoes, tomato purée, salt,
sugar and wine. Cover and simmer over low heat for 10 minutes, stirring once or twice.
Remove from hob and add
cream, thyme, parsley, cheese
and cooked pasta. Reheat very
gently, stirring until just hot,
and serve immediately.
Serves 6.

SPINACH, PINEAPPLE AND ROCKET SALAD WITH PECAN NUTS

An adventurous salad to please jaded palates. This one consists of layers of shredded spinach, spring onions, rocket and fresh pineapple with a topping of soured cream, yoghurt and pecan nuts. It can be made a few hours in advance, and refrigerated, and, because of the pineapple, it makes an excellent accompaniment to pork, turkey, duck or chicken. It is important to use very young, fresh spinach leaves, and, if rocket does not feature in your herb garden fresh basil may be substituted, using slightly less. The ingredients for this recipe can easily be doubled.

90 g (3 oz) finely shredded, bright spinach leaves*
half a bunch of spring onions, chopped
about 16 small stalks rocket
10 ml (2 tsp) lemon juice
25 ml (5 tsp) sunflower oil
25 ml (5 tsp) olive oil
pinch each of salt and sugar
half a small, sweet pineapple
60 ml (4 tbsp) cultured soured cream
60 ml (4 tbsp) thick Bulgarian yoghurt
10 ml (2 tsp) wholegrain mustard
5 ml (1 tsp) brown sugar
halved pecan nuts for garnish

Spread spinach over base of flattish salad bowl – a 23 cm (9 in) pie dish is just right. Sprinkle with spring onions. Tear rocket leaves coarsely, discarding stems; sprinkle over onions. Mix lemon juice, oils, salt and sugar, and pour over. Grate the peeled pineapple straight into the dish, using a coarse grater, and spread evenly. Mix soured cream, yoghurt, mustard and brown sugar and drizzle over pineapple.

Garnish prettily with pecan nuts, then cover and chill for about 3 hours, or overnight. Serves 4.

* Spinach needs to be washed in three lots of water. Remove ribs, spin dry, and shred.

BROCCOLI AND CUCUMBER SALAD WITH CREAMY DILL DRESSING

The sort of rich, crunchy salad which draws applause at summer luncheon buffets. Ladies love it. Good with cold meats and fish.

400 g (14 oz) broccoli, trimmed and sliced into thin 'trees'
half a cucumber, pared and julienned
toasted sunflower seeds for garnish

DRESSING
125 ml (4 fl oz) mayonnaise
125 ml (4 fl oz) thick Bulgarian yoghurt
2.5 ml (½ tsp) dried dill
pinch each of salt and sugar
2 spring onions, chopped
5 ml (1 tsp) wholegrain mustard

Cook broccoli in minimum amount of salted water until just tender and still a good colour. Drain if necessary and cool. Arrange broccoli and cucumber in a shallow salad dish.
Stir ingredients for dressing together until well combined. Spoon over cooled vegetables. (If not required immediately, cover and chill.) Garnish with a generous sprinkling of sunflower seeds just before serving. Serves 5–6.

VARIATION
Try the dill dressing on a platter of lightly cooked green beans, or mixed into boiled new potatoes.

WALNUT SALAD DRESSING

Although walnut oil has a very mild flavour, it has become fashionable to use it in salad dressings, despite the cost. It does add an indefinable flavour to a green salad, and if you add a handful of finely chopped walnuts (or pecans) to the greens, the flavour will be deliciously enhanced.

45 ml (3 tbsp) sunflower oil
45 ml (3 tbsp) walnut oil
20 ml (4 tsp) fresh lemon juice
1 clove garlic, crushed
small pinch of salt
1.25 ml (¼ tsp) mustard
   powder
15 ml (1 tbsp) finely chopped
   parsley

Place all the ingredients in a glass jar, close and shake until well combined and creamy.
Makes 125 ml (4 fl oz).

MIXED SALAD WITH SESAME DRESSING

A glistening mixture of greens and lentil sprouts with golden peppers. Super with chicken or pork dishes, and may be made several hours in advance and refrigerated.

1 very large or 2 medium
   yellow peppers (about 150 g
   (5 oz))*
60 g (2 oz) finely shredded
   young spinach leaves
half a bunch of spring onions,
   chopped
60 g (2 oz) finely shredded
   lettuce leaves
125 g (4 oz) lentil sprouts
125–250 g (4–9 oz) white
   mushrooms, wiped and sliced
   (optional)

DRESSING
45 ml (3 tbsp) sunflower oil
5 ml (1 tsp) dark sesame oil
25 ml (5 tsp) toasted sesame
   seeds
5 ml (1 tsp) brown sugar
15 ml (1 tbsp) lemon juice
10 ml (2 tsp) soy sauce

Mix all ingredients for dressing thoroughly, and then pour into a salad bowl.

Pour boiling water over peppers, place a weight on top to keep them submerged, leave for 5 minutes, then drain. Cut off tops, remove core and seeds, and slice into thin strips.

Add peppers to salad bowl, together with spinach, onions, lettuce, lentil sprouts and mushrooms, if using. Toss until shiny, then cover and chill for about 3 hours, or overnight.
Serves 6.

* To increase the flavour and digestibility of peppers, some cooks like to grill them, or put them on a hot radiant plate on the hob, until blistered and charred, then place them in a paper bag or a bowl of cold water, before removing skins and slicing. Personally, I am not happy with the concept of charred foods. In any case, if you have ever placed a pepper on a hot radiant plate and watched it jump and jerk, your sensitivities could be upset. I far prefer the boiling water method which is used in this recipe.

TOASTING SESAME SEEDS

To toast sesame seeds, place in a single layer in a non-stick frying pan and toss over low heat until golden brown, or bake on a biscuit tray in a moderate oven. In both cases take care that they do not scorch, which happens very easily. You can toast about 75 g (2½ oz) at a time. Store in a sealed glass jar.

HERBY WILD RICE, BROWN RICE AND MUSHROOM SALAD

Because wild rice is so expensive, it is often used in combination with other rice. Wild rice is actually the seed of a type of grass which grows in the shallow waters of certain lakes in North America. It is difficult to harvest, and this adds to the cost. The slim seeds look rather like little black gramophone needles, and have a nutty flavour and texture. There are different ways of cooking wild rice, but the brand I use can be successfully cooked together with brown rice, which simplifies the operation. The following is a multi-coloured salad which teams up well with cold meats, poultry or fish.

600 ml (1 pint) chicken stock
1 bouquet garni
100 g (3½ oz) wild rice, very well rinsed

100 g (3½ oz) brown rice
75 ml (5 tbsp) sunflower oil
15 g (½ oz) butter
250 g (9 oz) brown mushrooms, wiped and sliced
1–2 cloves garlic, crushed
1 large red pepper, cored, seeded and diced
2 small sprigs rosemary
250 g (9 oz) courgettes, pared and coarsely grated
5–6 slim spring onions, chopped
100 ml (7 tbsp) chopped parsley
15 ml (1 tbsp) lemon juice
25 ml (5 tsp) soy sauce
30 g (1 oz) shredded spinach leaves
bean sprouts of choice for garnish

Bring stock to the boil in a heavy-based saucepan. Add bouquet garni and both kinds of rice, stirring once to mix. As soon as stock returns to the boil, reduce heat to very low and simmer, covered, for 50–60 minutes,

until stock is absorbed. Remove bouquet garni.

Meanwhile, heat oil and butter in a large frying pan, add mushrooms, garlic, red pepper and rosemary, and stir-fry over medium heat until mushrooms are just starting to brown and shrink. Remove from hob and add remaining ingredients, except spinach. Toss to mix, then cover and set aside.

Tip hot, cooked rice into a large bowl. Remove rosemary sprigs from vegetable mixture and discard. Add vegetables to rice, together with any juices which might have formed while standing, and spinach. Toss well with a fork, cover loosely with a kitchen tea-towel so that steam can escape, and cool before serving, or refrigerate overnight.

To serve, pile onto a salad platter, and garnish with a sprinkling of sprouts.
Serves 6–8.

BOUQUET GARNI
These may be bought, ready for use, tied in convenient little muslin bags, or you can make your own by tying up a bay leaf, a sprig each of parsley and thyme in a square of muslin.

BULGUR
This is a fibre-rich, pre-cooked, cracked wheat which needs no further cooking if the fine-grained variety is used. For salads, simply soak it in water for 45 minutes, drain in a sieve and squeeze out all the moisture with your hands, and it is ready for use.
Take time to experiment with bulgur — it marries well with vegetables, herbs and spices. Toss soaked and squeezed bulgur with 45 ml (3 tbsp) lemony French dressing, and take it from there.

VINAIGRETTE WITH YOGHURT, TARRAGON AND WALNUT OIL

A subtly flavoured dressing which adds a special touch to any simple green salad.

5 ml (1 tsp) mustard powder
2 cloves garlic
2.5 ml (½ tsp) salt
30 ml (2 tbsp) tarragon vinegar
5 ml (1 tsp) dried tarragon
5 ml (1 tsp) sugar
1.25 ml (¼ tsp) paprika
45 ml (3 tbsp) walnut oil
200 ml (7 fl oz) sunflower oil
45 ml (3 tbsp) Bulgarian yoghurt

Place mustard powder, garlic, salt, vinegar, tarragon, sugar and paprika in blender and blend. Add remaining ingredients and blend until thoroughly combined, then chill. Shake or whisk before using.
Makes 300 ml (10 fl oz).

BULGUR SALAD WITH MUSHROOMS AND SPROUTS

A simply superb salad which goes with anything, but is particularly good served as part of a buffet meal, with cold chicken or fish, or even taking pride of place on a vegetarian platter, with the bulgur adding substance to the crunchy raw vegetables and lentil sprouts. This salad is quickly and easily prepared, and may be made in advance and chilled overnight.

180 g (6 oz) bulgur
250 g (9 oz) button mushrooms, wiped and sliced
8 slim spring onions, chopped
125 g (4 oz) lentil sprouts
200 g (7 oz) courgettes, pared and coarsely grated
45 ml (3 tbsp) toasted sesame seeds
15 g (½ oz) chopped parsley
pinch of salt

DRESSING
60 ml (4 tbsp) each sunflower and olive oil
5 ml (1 tsp) dark sesame oil
1 clove garlic, crushed
45 ml (3 tbsp) lemon juice
10 ml (2 tsp) pale, thin honey

Cover bulgur with water and leave to soak for about 45 minutes. Drain in a sieve and squeeze out all moisture with your hands. Combine with remaining salad ingredients.

Make dressing by mixing all ingredients, then toss with bulgur-and-vegetable mixture. Cover and chill.

To serve, spoon onto a large salad platter and garnish with whatever you fancy – thinly sliced avocado and tomatoes are good choices for added colour.
Serves 8.

BALSAMIC VINAIGRETTE

The king of vinegars, at a princely price – but for delicacy of flavour it is hard to beat. Years of maturing in a variety of wooden kegs result in a fragrant, mellow vinegar with gourmet appeal.

250 ml (8 fl oz) sunflower oil, or part sunflower and part olive oil
45 ml (3 tbsp) balsamic vinegar
10 ml (2 tsp) pale, thin honey
25 ml (5 tsp) finely chopped parsley
2.5 ml (½ tsp) paprika
45 ml (3 tbsp) claret, or red wine of choice
large pinch of salt
2.5 ml (½ tsp) mustard powder

Combine ingredients in a glass jar, close and shake well. Stand for at least 1 hour before using.
Makes about 350 ml (12 fl oz).

ITALIAN SALAD

This is a bold departure from the usual fresh and lightly flavoured salads which accompany most Italian meals. In this salad, the vegetables are poached, marinated in a dressing, and then topped with a gremolada-type mixture.

200 g (7 oz) very young, slim green beans, trimmed
200 g (7 oz) courgettes, pared
1 red pepper, cored, seeded and julienned
salt and milled black pepper

DRESSING
25 ml (5 tsp) sunflower oil
25 ml (5 tsp) olive oil
1.25 ml (¼ tsp) dried oregano
large pinch each of salt and sugar
15 ml (1 tbsp) lemon juice

TOPPING
15 g (½ oz) butter
10 ml (2 tsp) olive oil
30 g (1 oz) slightly stale, brown or white breadcrumbs
1 clove garlic, crushed
2.5 ml (½ tsp) finely grated lemon rind
15 ml (1 tbsp) grated Parmesan cheese
45 ml (3 tbsp) chopped parsley

Mix dressing ingredients and set aside.

Halve green beans if they're not as slim as bridge pencils. Slice courgettes into thin strips about same length as beans. Poach or steam beans, courgettes and red pepper until just cooked, drain if necessary, and arrange in a flattish, shallow serving dish. Season lightly and pour dressing over hot vegetables. Cover loosely and leave to cool.

To make topping, heat butter and oil in frying pan, add breadcrumbs and garlic, and toss over medium heat until crumbs are lightly browned and crisp. Remove from hob, mix in lemon rind, Parmesan and parsley, and sprinkle over salad just before serving.
Serves 4–6.

HINT
For best results buy virgin olive oil, in glass bottles.

GREEN BEAN, RED PEPPER AND SPROUT SALAD

This salad goes especially well with Chinese dishes or chicken.

100 ml (3½ fl oz) sunflower oil
5 ml (1 tsp) dark sesame oil
1 large onion, thinly sliced into rings
2 red peppers, cored, seeded and julienned
2 cloves garlic, crushed
400 g (14 oz) young green beans, trimmed and halved
45 ml (3 tbsp) soy sauce*
45 ml (3 tbsp) lemon juice
10 ml (2 tsp) pale, thin honey
225 g (8 oz) lentil sprouts
toasted almonds, sunflower or sesame seeds for garnish

Heat oils in a large frying pan, add onion, red peppers and garlic, and stir-fry for a few minutes until softening and onion turns golden yellow. Using a slotted spoon, transfer to a large, flattish salad bowl.

To frying pan, add beans, soy sauce, lemon juice and honey. Stir to mix, then cover and cook over low heat until tender. Add sprouts. Tip into mixture in salad bowl, tossing until everything is well combined and glistening.

Cover loosely, to avoid steaming, and leave for at least 1 hour to allow flavours to develop. Garnish just before serving. **Serves 8–10.**

* No salt has been included in the ingredients as the soy sauce should season the salad sufficiently.

HINT
Introduce a whiff of ginger by adding a little finely chopped peeled root ginger to the stir-fry.

CAULIFLOWER SALAD WITH MUSTARD DRESSING

Just a few ingredients go into making this excellent buffet salad. Because of the mustardy flavour, it teams up especially well with cold ham or pork, and may also be served in halved avocados for an unusual starter. Being a fairly rich, rather than a light, green salad, it is not suitable to serve with a creamy main course. It is most important to use tiny florets of cauliflower, without any woody base stems attached.

400–500 g (14–18 oz) small cauliflower florets
1 bunch of spring onions, chopped
125 g (4 oz) white mushrooms, wiped with lemon-water and thinly sliced
chopped walnuts for garnish

DRESSING
125 ml (4 fl oz) mayonnaise
125 ml (4 fl oz) thick Bulgarian yoghurt
5 ml (1 tsp) pale, thin honey
25 ml (5 tsp) wholegrain mustard

Soak cauliflower briefly in a bowl of cold, salted water to remove any grit, then rinse. Bring a large saucepan of salted water, with a dash of lemon juice, to the boil. Add cauliflower and allow water to return to a full boil. Drain, refresh under cold water; drain again. Toss cauliflower with spring onions and mushrooms; arrange in a large, shallow glass bowl to fit snugly.

Gently stir together ingredients for dressing until combined, then pour evenly over salad. Cover and refrigerate for 4–6 hours. Just before serving, scatter liberally with chopped walnuts. **Serves 6–8.**

ORANGE RICE SALAD WITH EASTERN SPICES

Rice salad is always one of the most popular items at a cold buffet, and the following is an interesting variation, particularly good with pork, ham or turkey. Because it is a very light salad, it may also be served with a creamy main dish such as Coronation Chicken. I like the nutty texture of brown rice, but long-grain white rice may be used.

60 ml (4 tbsp) sunflower oil
2 large leeks, finely shredded
5 ml (1 tsp) each ground
   coriander, cumin and ginger
1 stick cinnamon
4 whole cloves
250 g (9 oz) brown or long-
   grain white rice
500 ml (17 fl oz) water
125 ml (4 fl oz) fresh orange
   juice
60 g (2 oz) sultanas

5 ml (1 tsp) finely grated
   orange rind
2.5 ml (½ tsp) salt
4–6 spring onions, chopped
30 ml (2 tbsp) toasted sesame
   seeds
15 g (½ oz) butter
about 25 ml (5 tsp) French
   dressing
chopped coriander leaves or
   parsley for garnish

Heat oil, add leeks and spices, and sizzle over medium heat until aromatic and leeks have softened. Add rice, toss to mix, then add water, orange juice, sultanas, orange rind and salt. Bring to the boil, then cover and simmer over very low heat until liquid is absorbed and rice is cooked – about 25 minutes for white rice, or 50 minutes for brown. Remove cinnamon stick and cloves, and fork in onions, sesame seeds and butter.
   Tip into a salad bowl, cover loosely and cool. Serve at room temperature, or refrigerate

overnight. Just before serving, moisten with a little French dressing and garnish.
Serves 8.

GREEN BEAN, MUSHROOM AND SESAME SALAD

This is such a useful salad – tasty, attractive, prepared in minutes, and then left to cool while the flavours mingle, or chilled overnight.

500 g (18 oz) slim, young green
   beans, trimmed and sliced
2 large leeks, thinly sliced or
   shredded
125 g (4 oz) white mushrooms,
   wiped with lemon-water and
   thinly sliced
30 ml (2 tbsp) toasted sesame
   seeds
wedges of hard-boiled egg for
   garnish (optional)

DRESSING
25 ml (5 tsp) sherry vinegar or
   30 ml (2 tbsp) lemon juice
5 ml (1 tsp) Dijon mustard
10 ml (2 tsp) pale, thin honey
1.25 ml (¼ tsp) salt
100 ml (7 tbsp) sunflower oil
5–10 ml (1–2 tsp) dark
   sesame oil

Make dressing by whisking together all ingredients with a fork; leave to stand while preparing vegetables. Cook beans and leeks together in a little salted water until just tender, leaving lid of saucepan tilted to retain colour of beans. Drain (but do not refresh), then arrange in a large, shallow glass or porcelain salad bowl. Pour enough (about three-quarters) of dressing over to moisten vegetables. Add mushrooms; toss to mix, then set aside, lightly covered, to cool. Just before serving, toss in sesame seeds and tuck in egg wedges, if using.
Serves 6.

GREEN MAYONNAISE

Serve with poached leeks, asparagus or fish.

4 large spinach leaves, washed
a few tufts of parsley
2 spring onions, chopped
125 ml (4 fl oz) mayonnaise
1 small clove garlic, chopped

Boil spinach, parsley and onions in a little water for 3 minutes. Chop finely, or purée in a blender. Tip into a bowl, add mayonnaise and garlic, and mix well. (Do not purée mayonnaise with the spinach mixture as it will thin down too much.) Spoon into a glass jar and refrigerate.
Makes 125 ml (4 fl oz)

MARINATED MUSHROOM, FETA AND SPINACH SALAD

Here the perennially popular Greek salad is given a new twist with the addition of mushrooms and nuts, while the overnight marinating adds gusto to the completed dish. This boldly flavoured combination is super with Greek garlic lamb or any vegetarian dish with pulses or aubergines.

200 g (7 oz) feta cheese, rinsed and cubed
250 g (9 oz) white mushrooms, wiped and sliced
half a bunch of spring onions, chopped
2 red peppers, cored, seeded and diced
125 g (4 oz) shredded young spinach leaves
45 g (1½ oz) chopped pecan nuts, preferably toasted
1–2 tomatoes, sliced (optional)
about 45 ml (3 tbsp) French dressing
black olives for garnish

DRESSING
60 ml (4 tbsp) sunflower oil
60 ml (4 tbsp) olive oil
30 ml (2 tbsp) lemon juice
1 clove garlic, crushed
2.5 ml (½ tsp) dried oregano
2.5 ml (½ tsp) dried tarragon

Place cheese, mushrooms, spring onions and red peppers in a shallow glass or pottery bowl suitable for marinating.
 Mix all ingredients for the dressing. Pour over vegetables and toss to mix. Cover and marinate overnight in refrigerator.
 Turn mixture into a large shallow bowl, mix in spinach, nuts, tomatoes, if using, and just enough French dressing to add succulence. Garnish and serve.
Serves 8.

DEVILLED SALAD DRESSING WITH RED WINE

This dressing will add zest to any leafy greens, while the addition of sliced avocado and toasted sesame seeds make a really fine combination.

250 ml (8 fl oz) sunflower oil
25 ml (5 tsp) fresh lemon juice
60 ml (4 tbsp) full-bodied red wine
10 ml (2 tsp) Worcestershire sauce
25 ml (5 tsp) tomato sauce
5 ml (1 tsp) pale, thin honey
5 ml (1 tsp) wholegrain Dijon mustard
1–2 cloves garlic, peeled

Combine all ingredients in a glass jar, screw on cap and shake well. Stand at room temperature for a while before using, or refrigerate.
Makes about 375 ml (13 fl oz).

FRENCH PEAR FLAN

This pretty dessert of golden pastry and poached pears is glazed and then decorated with almonds.

PASTRY
100 g (3½ oz) soft butter
45 ml (3 tbsp) icing sugar
1 egg yolk, beaten
150 g (5 oz) pre-sifted plain (soft if available) flour
pinch of salt
10 ml (2 tsp) lemon juice

FILLING
750 g (1¾ lb) slightly underripe Packham's Triumph pears
250 ml (8 fl oz) water
75 g (2½ oz) caster sugar
1 stick cinnamon
3 whole cloves
10 ml (2 tsp) lemon juice
15 ml (1 tbsp) cornflour
15 ml (1 tbsp) Amaretto liqueur
blanched almonds to decorate

To make pastry, use an electric mixer to cream butter and icing sugar well. Beat in egg yolk, then flour sifted with a pinch of salt, and lemon juice. Beat until mixture holds together, shape into a ball, wrap in greaseproof paper and chill for 1 hour. Press evenly into a fluted flan tin. Work quickly so that dough remains cold. Prick all over, then place on a pre-heated baking tray and bake at 200 °C (400 °F, gas 6) for 12 minutes or until just beginning to colour. Cool.
  Peel, core and halve pears. Bring water, sugar, spices and lemon juice to the boil in a wide-based saucepan or frying pan. Boil for 5 minutes, then add pear halves, rounded sides up, in a single layer. Cover and poach gently until soft. Cool in syrup, then drain and slice thinly. Remove spices from syrup and pour into a small saucepan – you should have 250 ml (8 fl oz) syrup. Before heating, stir in cornflour slaked with a little

syrup and boil up, stirring, until thick and clear. Remove from heat and add liqueur.
  Sprinkle base of pastry case with 10 ml (2 tsp) caster sugar, to prevent it becoming soggy. Fill with sliced pears, arranged in concentric circles, then slowly spoon thickened syrup over. Tuck in an almond here and there; leave to cool and set.
Serves 8.

PEARS IN FILO BASKETS WITH AMARETTO SABAYON

If the title intimidates you, let me hasten to say that the filo baskets are optional, and the rest of this designer dessert is neither difficult nor time-consuming to prepare. The result, however, is guaranteed to impress discerning guests.

about 750 g (1¾ lb) slightly underripe Packham's Triumph pears
200 ml (7 fl oz) water
75 g (2½ oz) caster sugar
1 stick cinnamon
10 ml (2 tsp) lemon juice
chopped, toasted almonds to decorate

SABAYON
3 egg yolks
60 g (2 oz) caster sugar
5 ml (1 tsp) cornflour
45 ml (3 tbsp) Amaretto liqueur (it is important to use a top brand)
100 ml (3½ fl oz) whipping cream, whipped

Peel, halve and core pears. Bring water, sugar, cinnamon and lemon juice to the boil in a wide-based saucepan. Add pears in a single layer, rounded sides up, cover and poach gently until soft. Cool the pears in poaching liquid, then drain them well and chill.

To make sauce, put egg yolks, sugar and cornflour in the top of a small double boiler, or into a small saucepan set on top of a larger one and, using a balloon whisk, whisk until pale and thick. (Water in lower saucepan should be kept at simmering, not boiling point, otherwise mixture will scramble. However, it should not be under-cooked either, or it will separate on standing, so go carefully here.) Slowly add liqueur and, using a wooden spoon, stir until mixture thickens again – it should be creamy and the colour of butter-scotch. Pour into a smallish container, cool, and chill. Just before serving fold in cream.

To serve, place one pear half, rounded side up, on each serving plate, or nestle it in a filo basket (see box). Pour over enough of the sabayon to coat. If liked, sprinkle a few chopped, toasted almonds over tops; serve at once. **The sabayon is enough for 10–12 small pear halves.**

FILO BASKETS
To make filo baskets, brush large, deep muffin tins with butter, and lightly press in a square of filo, using only one layer. Brush with melted butter and top with another square. Brush with butter. Do not attempt to make a tidy little basket – the edges will be uneven. Bake at 200 °C (400 °F, gas 6) for about 5 minutes, until richly browned, then simply lift out of tins and cool on a wire rack, where (unless it is a wet day) they will remain crisp for several hours. If liked, you can neaten edges by snipping with a pair of kitchen scissors.

Extra-large eggs have been used in the recipes throughout this book – in most cases the correct results will not be achieved if smaller eggs are used.

TIRAMISÚ

This is a wickedly rich and potent Italian dessert, usually made with mascarpone – a dessert cream cheese. It may be flavoured, in Tiramisú, with liqueur, brandy or rum. As mascarpone is not always freely available, I have substituted cream cheese. For a lighter dessert, Ricotta may be substituted but use slightly less rum.

250 g (9 oz) cream cheese or Ricotta
125 g (4 oz) sponge finger (boudoir) biscuits
250 ml (8 fl oz) warm water
15 ml (1 tbsp) pure, instant coffee granules
25–30 ml (5–6 tsp) dark rum
3 eggs, separated
100 g (3¹/₂ oz) caster sugar
a few drops of vanilla extract
75–100 g (2¹/₂ – 3¹/₂ oz) dark chocolate, finely grated
cocoa powder

If using cream cheese, tip into a fine sieve and refrigerate overnight to allow any excess moisture to drain off. Break biscuits into three and place in a single layer in base of serving dish, preferably a deep-sided pie dish, with a diameter of about 23 cm (9 in). Mix water, coffee and rum and pour slowly over biscuits. Whisk egg yolks with half the sugar until pale and thick. Using a wooden spoon, stir in cheese and vanilla. Mix well but do not beat – it is better to have a few small lumps than to over-mix. Whisk egg whites until stiff. Gradually beat in remaining sugar and beat until glossy. Fold into cheese mixture. Sprinkle chocolate evenly over biscuits. Pour cheese mixture over the chocolate – the mixture will be fairly thick, but should spread quite easily to cover the chocolate completely. Sieve a little cocoa powder over the top and chill for at least 5 hours. **Serves 8.**

ORANGE BAVAROIS WITH CHOCOLATE SAUCE

Set in individual ramekins, unmoulded and drizzled with chocolate-liqueur sauce, this is a beautiful dessert. The warm sauce with the chilled little puddings is a stylish trend, and advance preparation makes it an excellent choice for entertaining.

Although the addition of egg whites is not traditional, they do help to lighten the rich custard.

15 ml (1 tbsp) gelatine
125 ml (4 fl oz) fresh orange juice
375 ml (13 fl oz) milk
finely grated rind of 1 medium orange
2 eggs, separated
60 ml (4 tbsp) caster sugar
a few drops of vanilla extract
125 ml (4 fl oz) whipping cream, whipped

SAUCE
100 g (3¹/₂ oz) milk chocolate (not white or plain*), broken up
45 ml (3 tbsp) single cream or evaporated milk
25 ml (5 tsp) orange flavoured liqueur

Using a small container, sprinkle gelatine onto orange juice and leave to sponge. Scald milk with orange rind – do this slowly, over low heat, to release flavour of rind. Whisk egg yolks with sugar until pale and thick. Strain hot milk onto egg mixture, stir to mix, then return to saucepan and cook as for custard – either in a double boiler, or over very low heat, stirring, until it coats the back of a wooden spoon. Remove from heat and add sponged gelatine and vanilla. Stir to dissolve gelatine, then cool and chill until thickened – do not allow it to start setting. Fold in cream. Whisk egg whites stiffly with a pinch of salt. Using a metal spoon, stir a spoon or two through mixture, then fold in remainder. Pour into eight rinsed ramekins (or one large mould, if preferred) and chill for several hours until set.

To make sauce, melt chocolate and cream in a small double boiler or saucepan over very low heat, stirring occasionally until smooth. Do not allow to boil or bubble. It may now be set aside and gently reheated when required, with the liqueur added just before serving.

Unmould ramekins onto individual serving plates by running a knife round sides. Drizzle a little sauce over each mould, allowing it to run down sides. You need not use all the sauce. Serve immediately.
Serves 8.

* Plain chocolate will overpower the delicate orange flavour of the dessert.

PORT AND PECAN CHIFFON PIE

There are countless versions of these so-called pies, consisting of a sweet, flavoured custard enriched with cream, lightened with egg whites and set in a pastry or crumb crust. This one is a slightly tipsy favourite, and the method used will appeal to cooks who are nervous of gelatine: all the ingredients for the basic custard are simply heated together, making it uncomplicated and flop-proof.

CRUST
100 g (3¹/₂ oz) sweet biscuit crumbs
45 ml (3 tbsp) finely chopped pecan nuts
75–100 g (2¹/₂ – 3¹/₂ oz) melted butter

FILLING
3 eggs, separated
500 ml (17 fl oz) milk
pinch of salt

45 ml (3 tbsp) sugar
15 ml (1 tbsp) gelatine plus an extra pinch
125 ml (4 fl oz) cream
few drops of vanilla extract
25 ml (5 tsp) caster sugar
45 ml (3 tbsp) tawny port
45 ml (3 tbsp) finely chopped pecan nuts*
whipped cream, chocolate curls, or simply a dusting of cinnamon to decorate

Make crust by mixing all the ingredients, using just enough butter to bind. Press onto base of a greased 20 cm (18 in) pie dish. Bake at 160 ˚C (325 ˚F, gas 3) for 15 minutes. Set aside to cool while making filling. (You can make the crust days in advance, when your oven is on anyway, and refrigerate.)

To make the filling, whisk egg yolks with milk and salt and pour into top of double boiler. Add 45 ml (3 tbsp) sugar and gelatine and heat over gently simmering water, stirring, until

mixture thickens like custard. Pour into a bowl, give it a quick whisk, cool and either chill or stir over iced water until beginning to set. Whip cream softly with vanilla and fold into custard mixture. Whisk egg whites until fairly stiff, gradually add caster sugar and whisk until glossy. Using a metal spoon, stir a few spoonfuls through the custard mixture, and fold in the remainder. Finally fold in port and pecans. Pour into crust and chill until set.

Decorate before serving.
Serves 8.

* Lightly toasting pecan nuts brings out the flavour.

VARIATION
BRANDY AND GINGER CHIFFON PIE
Make as above, but omit port and pecans. Substitute 30–40 ml (2–2¹/₂ tbsp) brandy and 1–2 walnut-sized knobs preserved ginger, finely chopped.

PEACH AND APPLE CRUMBLE

A homely dessert, combining canned peaches and fresh apples.

900 g (2 lb) canned peaches, sliced, plus the syrup
2 medium Golden Delicious apples, peeled and sliced
45 g (1½ oz) sultanas
45 ml (3 tbsp) orange-flavoured liqueur
finely grated rind of ½ an orange

CRUMBLE
150 g (5 oz) plain (soft if available) flour
5 ml (1 tsp) baking powder
1.25 ml (¼ tsp) salt
7.5 ml (1½ tsp) ground mixed spice
75 g (2½ oz) caster sugar
30 g (1 oz) desiccated coconut
45 g (1½ oz) chopped pecan nuts
100 g (3½ oz) butter

Spoon peaches and their syrup into a deep, 23 cm (9 in) pie dish. Add apples, sultanas, liqueur and orange rind, and toss to mix.

To make crumble, sift flour, baking powder, salt and mixed spice. Add sugar, coconut and nuts. Rub in butter until crumbly and sprinkle over fruit to form a thick, even layer. Bake at 180 °C (350 °F, gas 4) for 30–35 minutes. (This pie may be made in advance and heated through at 160 °C (325 °F, gas 3).)
Serves 6–8.

MEXICAN RUM CUSTARDS

Closely related to Crème Caramel, but with a subtle twist to the flavour. Slow baking and a rich custard ensure a perfect, butter-smooth texture, making this a dessert to be lingered over.

CARAMEL
150 g (5 oz) granulated sugar
100 ml (3½ fl oz) water

CUSTARD
400 g (14 oz) canned evaporated milk
500 ml (17 fl oz) milk
4 eggs
pinch of salt
a few drops of vanilla extract
45 ml (3 tbsp) dark rum
75 g (2½ oz) caster sugar

To make caramel, place sugar and water in a saucepan with a long handle, and stir over medium heat until sugar has dissolved, then boil without stirring until medium caramel in colour. Shake pan occasionally to allow syrup to brown evenly, and be careful not to let it darken – this can happen in a flash. Remove from heat just before you think it is necessary, as it will continue browning even while you're lining moulds. Working quickly, pour into 8-10 small ovenproof ramekins, swirling to coat base and as much of sides as syrup will cover. Set aside to cool.

To make custard, heat milks together but do not boil. Beat eggs with salt, vanilla, rum and sugar. Pour on hot milk, stirring, then strain into caramel-lined moulds. Place moulds in a large roasting tin, not touching each other (or they could crack), and fill roasting tin with hot water to reach two-thirds up sides of moulds. Bake on middle shelf of oven at 150 °C (300 °F, gas 2) for 45–50 minutes until just set – any slight wobbles will firm up on cooling. Cool in bain marie, then remove and chill overnight.

Unmould onto individual serving plates. There is no need for decoration – caramel will run down and form a pool under each custard – simplicity of presentation is part of the appeal of this popular dessert.
Serves 8–10.

CHIFFON PUMPKIN PIE

A light version of baked pumpkin pie with a spicy filling.

CRUST
100 g (3½ oz) ginger biscuit
    crumbs
75 g (2½ oz) melted butter

FILLING
500 g (18 oz) peeled and cubed
    pumpkin (peeled weight)
2.5 ml (½ tsp) ground
    cinnamon
1.25 ml (¼ tsp) ground
    nutmeg
small pinch of ground cloves
60 ml (4 tbsp) caster sugar
20 ml (4 tsp) golden syrup
2 egg yolks
10 ml (2 tsp) cornflour
15 ml (1 tbsp) gelatine
45 ml (3 tbsp) fresh orange
    juice
125 ml (4 fl oz) whipping
    cream, whipped
4 egg whites, lightly whisked
ground cinnamon, and
    whipped cream

Make crust by mixing crumbs
and butter. Press onto base of
greased 20 cm (8 in) pie dish
and chill.

To make filling, boil pumpkin
in a little lightly salted water –
use minimum necessary to prevent scorching – 125 ml (4 fl oz)
should be plenty. When cooked,
drain very well and purée in a
blender, until smooth – you
should have 500 ml (17 fl oz)
purée. Spoon into a heavy-based
saucepan and add spices, sugar,
syrup and egg yolks beaten with
cornflour. Stir over low heat until
mixture is cooked and thickened.
Meanwhile, sponge gelatine in
orange juice. Stir into hot pumpkin mixture and stir until dissolved, then pour into a mixing
bowl and set aside to cool. Fold
in cream and stir a few teaspoonfuls of egg white through mixture, then fold in the remainder.
At first mixture may curdle
slightly, but it should smooth
out as you continue to fold.

Pour filling into chilled crust,
dust with cinnamon, and
refrigerate for about 8 hours.
Decorate with whipped cream,
lightly flavoured with grated
orange rind.
Serves 8.

FRUIT FLAN WITH CRÈME PÂTISSIÈRE

An essential part of every cook's repertoire – not only because it is a classically popular dessert, but because it is hard to beat for dramatic eye-appeal. In this version, scarlet glazed strawberries and kiwi fruit are arranged on a base of thick confectioner's custard, smoothed into a rich shortcrust pastry case. Once assembled and decorated this jewel-bright flan always draws applause, and yet, despite its professional appearance, it is not at all tricky to make. The following is a basic version, but the custard may be flavoured with orange or lemon rind instead of vanilla, and the cream topping may have a dash of complementary liqueur.

PROCESSOR PASTRY
100 g (3½ oz) soft butter, diced
25 ml (5 tsp) icing sugar
1 egg yolk
150 g (5 oz) plain (soft if available) flour
pinch of salt
10 ml (2 tsp) lemon juice

CUSTARD FILLING
500 ml (17 fl oz) milk
2 whole eggs and 1 yolk (reserve white for brushing pastry)
30 ml (2 tbsp) plain flour (soft if available)
30 ml (2 tbsp) cornflour
45 ml (3 tbsp) caster sugar
pinch of salt
a few drops of vanilla extract

TOPPING
150 g (5 oz) strawberries, hulled, rinsed, dried and halved
1–2 kiwi fruit, peeled and sliced into thin rings

GLAZE
15 ml (1 tbsp) strawberry jam melted with 5 ml (1 tsp) water
whipped cream to decorate

To make pastry, place all ingredients, except lemon juice, in a food processor fitted with grinding blade and process until finely crumbed. Add lemon juice and process until mixture just forms a soft ball. Wrap and chill for 1 hour.

Meanwhile, make custard by scalding milk. Whisk together eggs, extra yolk, plain flour, cornflour, sugar and salt. Pour on hot milk, stir to mix, then return to saucepan. Stir over medium heat, using a wooden spoon, then as mixture starts to thicken, whisk with a balloon whisk until very thick and smooth, allowing mixture to bubble for a minute or two to cook flour. Add the vanilla, give a final good whisk, pour into a bowl, drape a piece of waxed paper over top to prevent a skin from forming, and cool.

Press chilled pastry into a 23 cm (9 in) fluted, loose-bottomed flan ring. (It is not necessary to roll out this pastry, simply press out evenly with your fingers – it will just cover base and sides thinly.) Prick base and sides all over with a fork, and bake at 180 °C (350 °F, gas 4) on middle shelf of oven for 12–15 minutes, until palest beige. Remove and cool. (This pastry case may be made the day before and stored in an airtight container.) Carefully remove flan ring, and place case on a large, flat serving plate. Brush base with a little softly beaten egg white, to keep it crisp. Dry for a few minutes before spooning in cold custard. Level top, and arrange strawberry halves, rounded sides up, and kiwi fruit in concentric circles, leaving a border round edge for cream. Using a pastry brush, paint strawberries with glaze. Chill for about 4 hours – although it can, at a pinch, be left overnight.

Before serving, decorate with rosettes of whipped cream.
Serves 8.

RUM AND LYCHEE TRIFLE

A far cry from the old sherry and jelly combination, this trifle has an exotic combination of flavours. Nevertheless it is easily prepared, using a bought sponge, a simple custard, and a can of fruit.

1 x 200 g (7 oz) sponge layer, about 18 cm (7 in) round and 4 cm (1½ in) deep
400 g (14 oz) canned lychees, drained and juice reserved
45 ml (3 tbsp) dark rum
25 ml (5 tsp) cornflour
375 ml (13 fl oz) milk
45 ml (3 tbsp) caster sugar
2 egg yolks, beaten
a few drops of vanilla extract
whipped cream to decorate

Cut sponge to cover base of a 20 cm (8 in) glass dish or bowl – the flatter the base the better. Mix 100 ml (3½ fl oz) of the lychee syrup with 15 ml (1 tbsp) of rum, and pour over sponge. Remove stones from lychees, slice flesh thinly, and arrange on top of sponge.

To make custard, mix cornflour, milk and sugar in saucepan, and stir over medium heat until thickened. Pour onto yolks, then return to saucepan and stir over low heat just until eggs are cooked – do not boil. Remove and stir in remaining rum and vanilla. Pour over lychees in an even layer. (Custard will seem unusually thick, but thins out slightly in refrigerator.) Cool, and refrigerate, preferably overnight.

Before serving, decorate with piped whipped cream and if you have a fresh kiwi fruit or a few strawberries, use one or other for colour, but avoid using decorations such as glacé cherries and angelica on this trifle.
Serves 6–8.

EGGLESS CHOCOLATE ORANGE DESSERT

Despite the fact that this dessert contains neither eggs nor block chocolate, it is beautifully light and smooth and makes an excellent alternative to a mousse, especially after a rich meal. Set it in a glass serving bowl, or in wine glasses.

10 ml (2 tsp) gelatine
125 ml (4 fl oz) cold water
30 ml (2 tbsp) cocoa powder
2.5 ml (½ tsp) finely grated orange rind (half a small orange)
100 g (3½ oz) caster sugar
125 ml (4 fl oz) fresh orange juice
175 g (6 oz) canned evaporated milk, chilled overnight
a few drops of lemon juice
125 ml (4 fl oz) whipping cream
a few drops of vanilla extract
extra whipped cream and chocolate curls or sifted cocoa powder to decorate

Sprinkle gelatine onto water in a small saucepan and allow to sponge for a few minutes. Add cocoa powder, orange rind, sugar and orange juice and stir over low heat just until gelatine and sugar have dissolved – do not overheat, and certainly do not boil. Remove from hob and cool, then strain into small bowl (don't omit this step or orange rind will spoil texture) and chill briefly until thickening. In a large, chilled mixing bowl whisk evaporated milk with lemon juice until very thick and trebled in volume. Slowly add cold cocoa mixture, whisking constantly. Whip cream with vanilla, and fold in, using a metal spoon. Spoon into 6–8 glasses, or a bowl with a capacity of at least 1.25 litres (2¼ pints), and chill until set. Decorate.
Serves 6–8.

VANILLA CREAMS WITH STRAWBERRY COULIS

Because the dreamy dessert, coeur à la crème, requires perforated heart-shaped moulds – a factor which daunts cooks with only basic equipment, I have devised a much simpler version using similar ingredients, but with the addition of a little gelatine which means the mixture may be set in ordinary ramekins, or even one large mould. Once unmoulded, the snow-white fluffy creams are sparked with a fresh strawberry sauce spiked with maraschino. The result is an eye-catching dessert in festive colours. The texture is that of a light cheesecake, without a crust or egg yolks.

250 ml (8 fl oz) whipping cream
250 g (9 oz) curd cheese, or cream cheese for a richer result*
a few drops vanilla extract**
15 ml (1 tbsp) gelatine
45 ml (3 tbsp) cold water
2 egg whites
75 g (2¹/₂ oz) caster sugar
8 perfect, sugared strawberries to decorate

STRAWBERRY COULIS
250 g (9 oz) ripe strawberries, hulled, rinsed and sliced
45 ml (3 tbsp) caster sugar
30–45 ml (2–3 tbsp) maraschino liqueur (optional)***

Whip cream, then beat in cheese and vanilla. Sponge gelatine in water, and dissolve over low heat. Allow to cool slightly without jelling. Using an electric whisk, drizzle gelatine slowly into cream mixture, whisking constantly. Whisk egg whites until soft peaks form, then slowly whisk in sugar until glossy, like meringue. Gently fold mixtures together until combined. Pour into eight ramekins or one large mould, levelling tops with back of a spoon. Chill until set.

To make coulis, place strawberries in a blender goblet, sprinkle with sugar, then stand for about 20 minutes to draw juices. Blend until smooth. Pour into a container and chill.

To serve, unmould ramekins onto individual serving plates, or large mould onto platter. Stir liqueur, if using, into strawberry purée and pour over or around the creams. Top each mould with one perfect, sugared berry. **Serves 8.**

* Have cheese at room temperature to avoid gelatine setting immediately.

** Or omit vanilla and use vanilla-flavoured sugar in meringue.

*** If omitting maraschino, you may wish to add a little extra sugar.

CHOCOLATE WHISKY MOUSSE WITH PEARS

Most cooks will have a recipe for chocolate mousse – a dreamy dessert, combining chocolate, eggs and cream. The following version is a little different: it is lighter (half soured cream is used) and includes a surprise in the shape of pears. Not only do chocolate and pears have a natural affinity for each other, but the fruit cuts the richness of the pudding, and also makes it possible to sneak in two extra servings. Adding the minimum amount of gelatine to the chocolate mixture ensures that it will blanket the pears completely, while the texture nevertheless remains soft and creamy. Use individual glass serving bowls and either fresh or canned pears.

8 small poached pear halves or 900 g (2 lb) canned pear halves

100 g (3¹/₂ oz) bar plain
   chocolate
10 ml (2 tsp) pure, instant
   coffee granules
25 ml (5 tsp) water
3 eggs, separated
about 45 ml (3 tbsp) whisky
5 ml (1 tsp) gelatine
60 ml (4 tbsp) reserved pear
   syrup
125 ml (4 fl oz) cultured soured
   cream
125 ml (4 fl oz) whipping
   cream, whipped with a few
   drops of vanilla extract
lightly sweetened whipped
   cream and chocolate curls to
   decorate

Drain pears well, reserving syrup,
and place one half, rounded side
up, in each of eight serving
bowls. Break up chocolate,
except for two squares, joined.
Draw a potato peeler, dipped
into hot water, down the long
side of these two squares to
make fine curls (or shave carefully with a sharp knife). Set

aside. Place remaining chocolate,
coffee and water in a small container and melt over simmering
water – do not allow to get too
hot. Using a hand-held, electric
mixer, whisk egg yolks and
whisky very well. Add melted
chocolate and whisk until thoroughly combined. Using same
container as used to melt chocolate, sponge gelatine briefly in
reserved pear syrup
(60 ml (4 tbsp)), then dissolve
over low heat, and whisk into
chocolate mixture. Stir in soured
cream, then fold in whipped
cream. Whisk egg whites fairly
stiffly with a pinch of salt. Stir a
few spoonfuls through the mixture, and then fold in remainder.
Chill until just beginning to set,
then spoon equally over pears to
cover completely and return to
refrigerator to firm. Decorate just
before serving.
Serves 8.

RUM AND ORANGE FRUIT TART

125 g (4 oz) pitted dates,
   chopped
60 g (2 oz) mixed dried fruit
5 ml (1 tsp) bicarbonate of
   soda
250 ml (8 fl oz) boiling water
125 g (4 oz) plain (soft if
   available) flour
pinch of salt
5 ml (1 tsp) baking
   powder
5 ml (1 tsp) ground mixed
   spice
60 g (2 oz) soft butter
75 g (2¹/₂ oz) caster sugar
1 egg, beaten

SYRUP
200 ml (7 fl oz) fresh orange
   juice
75 g (2¹/₂ oz) granulated sugar
15 g (¹/₂ oz) butter
45–60 ml (3–4 tbsp) dark rum
   (60 ml (4 tbsp) makes it very
   potent)

Mix dates and dried fruit.
Sprinkle in bicarbonate of soda,
pour boiling water over, stir to
mix, then leave to cool completely. Sift flour, salt, baking
powder and spice. Cream butter
and sugar well. Whisk in egg,
together with a teaspoon of flour
mixture. The mixture may
curdle, but it matters not. Add
fruit mixture, then fold in flour
mixture, combining thoroughly.
Turn into a lightly oiled, deep,
20 cm (8 in) pie dish, and bake
at 180 °C (350 °F, gas 4) for
25–30 minutes until risen and
richly browned.

   Meanwhile, make syrup by
mixing orange juice, sugar and
butter in a saucepan. Bring to
the boil, stirring, then boil rapidly, uncovered, for 3 minutes.
Remove from hob and add rum.
Prick the hot tart all over with a
skewer and slowly pour the
syrup over. Leave for 24 hours
before serving.
Serves 8–10.

BRANDIED APPLE CINNAMON CHEESECAKE

This is a very light and refreshing cheesecake, which may also be made without the crust and set in small ramekins to be unmoulded and decorated before serving. Best made a day in advance.

CRUST
175 g (6 oz) sweet biscuit crumbs (petit beurre biscuits are a good choice)
100 g (3½ oz) melted butter
2.5 ml (½ tsp) ground cinnamon

FILLING
375 g (13 oz) canned unsweetened apple pie filling
2 eggs, separated
75 g (2½ oz) caster sugar
25 ml (5 tsp) pale, thin honey
25 ml (5 tsp) brandy (optional)
250 g (9 oz) curd cheese
15–20 ml (3–4 tsp) gelatine*
45 ml (3 tbsp) cold water
125 ml (4 fl oz) whipping cream, whipped with 2.5 ml (½ tsp) ground cinnamon
whipped cream and extra ground cinnamon to decorate

Mix ingredients for crust and press onto base of 23 cm (9 in) greased pie dish. Chill while making filling, or bake for 10 minutes at 160 °C (325 °F, gas 3) and cool.

To make filling, place apple, egg yolks, sugar, honey and brandy, if using, in a blender goblet and blend until perfectly smooth. Spoon cheese into mixing bowl and whisk in apple purée. Sponge gelatine in water, dissolve over low heat and slowly whisk into cheese mixture. Fold in whipped cream, and then egg whites whisked with a pinch of salt. Pour onto crust, or into rinsed moulds, and chill, preferably overnight. Decorate cheesecake with a lattice of cream and dust with extra cinnamon; or turn out if moulded, and then decorate.
Serves 10.

* The amount of gelatine depends on how juicy the apples are – if not packed solid, use 20 ml (4 tsp).

TOFFEE COFFEE MOUSSE

Sheer, delicious indulgence and the epitome of all that is rich, sweet and forbidden.

100 g (3¹/₂ oz) granulated sugar
60 ml (4 tbsp) water
250 ml (8 fl oz) milk
3 eggs, separated
10 ml (2 tsp) pure, instant coffee granules
10 ml (2 tsp) gelatine
30 ml (2 tbsp) water
125 ml (4 fl oz) cultured soured cream
a few drops of vanilla extract
125 ml (4 fl oz) whipping cream, softly whipped
coarsely crushed toasted walnuts or pecan nuts to decorate

Combine sugar and water in saucepan, stir over low heat until sugar dissolves, brushing down sides, and then boil rapidly, uncovered, until a rich caramel in colour. Watch carefully, and shake saucepan occasionally so that it does not scorch in spots, and do not allow to burn or darken. Remove from hob and slowly add milk – take care as mixture will spatter. Return to hob, and stir over low heat to melt caramel, which will have set into a brittle ball, but which will slowly melt again. When completely dissolved, pour onto egg yolks which have been whisked with coffee granules, then return to saucepan and stir over low heat until custard thickens. Do not boil. Remove from hob and, if coffee has not dissolved completely, give custard a quick whisk. Sprinkle gelatine onto water, sponge for a minute, add to hot custard and stir until dissolved. Cool and then chill until just beginning to set. Stir in soured cream and vanilla, and then fold in cream. Whisk egg whites. Using a metal spoon, stir a little through coffee mixture before folding in remainder. Pour into 5–6 glasses and return to refrigerator to set. Sprinkle with nuts before serving. **Serves 5–6.**

FRUIT SALAD WITH YOGHURT AND PECANS

Mangoes predominate in this summery dessert. The yoghurt-soured cream dressing and the topping of crunchy nuts elevate it to dinner party fare. Prepare in advance, but serve on the same day.

1.25 kg (2¹/₂ lb) ripe, fibreless mangoes, peeled and cubed (weighed after removing peel and pips)
6 rings sweet, fresh pineapple, finely diced
4 bananas, thinly sliced and tossed in lemon juice

YOGHURT CREAM
125 ml (4 fl oz) thick, cultured soured cream
250 ml (8 fl oz) thick Bulgarian yoghurt
2.5 ml (¹/₂ tsp) finely grated orange rind
25 ml (5 tsp) pale, thin honey
15 ml (1 tbsp) dark rum (optional)

BUTTERED PECANS
15 g (¹/₂ oz) butter
20 ml (4 tsp) dark, soft brown sugar
20 ml (4 tsp) water
45 g (1¹/₂ oz) coarsely chopped pecan nuts

Place fruits in a deep bowl. Mix all ingredients for yoghurt cream; pour over. Cover; chill for 4–6 hours. To make topping, melt butter, sugar and water. Add nuts; toss over low heat for about 5 minutes, until crunchy. Drain on paper towels. Sprinkle over dessert just before serving. **Serves 8.**

MOCHA CHOCOLATE CHEESECAKE

A smooth, silky cheesecake which may be made a day in advance and refrigerated.

PROCESSOR PASTRY CRUST
90 g (3 oz) plain (soft if available) flour
25 ml (5 tsp) cocoa powder
15 ml (1 tbsp) caster sugar
60 g (2 oz) cold butter, diced
1.25 ml (¼ tsp) baking powder

FILLING
250 g (9 oz) curd cheese
75 g (2½ oz) caster sugar
2 eggs, separated
a few drops of vanilla extract
100 g (3½ oz) bar plain chocolate
75 ml (5 tbsp) water
10 ml (2 tsp) pure, instant coffee granules

10 ml (2 tsp) gelatine
125 ml (4 fl oz) whipping cream, whipped
shaved chocolate and/or whipped cream to decorate

To make crust, place all ingredients in a food processor fitted with grinding blade and process very well until mixture is thoroughly combined, moist and fine. Using back of a spoon, press down firmly onto base only of a deep, lightly oiled 20 cm (8 in) cake tin with a removable base. Bake at 180 ˚C (350 ˚F, gas 4) for 15 minutes. Cool before adding filling.
   To make filling, use a hand-held electric mixer to whisk together cheese, 45 ml (3 tbsp) of sugar and egg yolks. When smooth, beat in vanilla. Break up chocolate, place in small container with 25 ml (5 tsp) of water and coffee, and place over simmering water. Do not overheat – chocolate should just soften without melting. Slowly whisk

chocolate into cheese mixture. Soften gelatine in same container in remaining water, dissolve over low heat, then slowly dribble into cheese mixture, beating all the time. Wash and dry beaters, then whisk egg whites until stiff. Gradually beat in remaining sugar and whisk until glossy. Stir about 30 ml (2 tbsp) into cheese mixture, then fold in remainder, together with cream. (Stirring a little meringue mixture into cheese mixture makes it easier to fold in remainder without over-mixing.) Mix gently but thoroughly, then pour into crust and refrigerate overnight. Decorate before serving.
Serves 8.

VARIATION
A crumb crust may be substituted for the pastry base. Use 100 g (3½ oz) biscuit crumbs mixed with 75 g (2½ oz) melted butter and 10 ml (2 tsp) cocoa powder, and use to line the base.

IRISH COFFEE CHOCOLATE ROULADE

Notorious for its wicked, wanton richness, chocolate roulade is a meltingly soft mixture of eggs, sugar, chocolate and cream, rather like a deflated soufflé. In this recipe it is laced with whisky to compound the felony further. Always serve a fruit salad alongside, for guests who would rather not indulge in such decadence.

ROULADE
4 eggs, separated
100 g (3½ oz) caster sugar
100 g (3½ oz) plain chocolate
45 ml (3 tbsp) water
10 ml (2 tsp) pure, instant coffee granules
10 ml (2 tsp) cocoa powder

FILLING
200 ml (7 fl oz) cream
15 ml (1 tbsp) whisky

5 ml (1 tsp) instant coffee
granules
15 ml (1 tbsp) icing sugar and
a few drops of vanilla extract

Brush a 33 x 20 cm (13 x 8 in)
Swiss roll tin with oil and line
with greaseproof (not waxed)
paper, also brushed with oil. (It
is important that the tin be at
least 2 cm (3/4 in) deep, as
roulade will puff up dramatically
in oven, although it deflates on
cooling.) Whisk egg yolks, slowly
add caster sugar, whisking until
pale. Break up chocolate and
place in small container with
water, coffee and cocoa powder.
Melt over low heat, cool slightly,
then whisk into yolk mixture.
When well combined, fold in
egg whites, stiffly whisked with a
pinch of salt. Pour into lined tin
and bake at 180 °C (350 °F, gas 4)
for 15 minutes, then at 160 °C
(325 °F, gas 3) for 5 minutes –
roulade should be just firm and
springy to the touch; overbaking
will cause it to crack when

rolling*. Cover immediately
with a damp cloth, cool and
then chill for at least 6 hours.
To turn out, trim edges with a
sharp knife, invert onto a sheet
of waxed paper dusted with
cocoa powder, and peel off
baking paper.
    Whisk all ingredients for filling
until cream stiffens – this takes
longer than usual, because of the
whisky, but any good cream will
thicken. Use an electric whisk if
possible. Spread over roulade
and, with the help of the paper,
roll up carefully from long side
and slide onto a large, flat serving platter. Dust top with icing
sugar, chill; serve in thin slices.
Serves 8–10.

* I have a fine remedy for a
roulade with a badly cracked
top. Carefully flip it over – the
bottom side will be smooth –
ease out paper, then dust with
icing sugar. Voilà!

AMARETTO CREAM

*This is a versatile dessert with an
alluring flavour and the texture and
colour of silky snow. It is a seduc-
tively rich indulgence, and although
it can be served as a cheesecake (see
Variation), it is more elegant
swirled into long-stemmed glasses,
while a cluster of lychees and toasted almonds complements the
liqueur to perfection.*

250 g (9 oz) cream or curd
cheese
25 ml (5 tsp) pale, thin honey
45 ml (3 tbsp) caster sugar
30–45 ml (2–3 tbsp) Amaretto
liqueur
a few drops of vanilla extract
10 ml (2 tsp) gelatine
30 ml (2 tbsp) cold water
200 ml (7 fl oz) whipping
cream, whipped
2 egg whites, stiffly whisked
fresh or canned lychees, stones
removed, and slivers of
toasted almonds to decorate

Whisk together cheese, honey,
sugar, liqueur and vanilla.
Sponge gelatine in water, dissolve over low heat, and slowly
dribble into cheese mixture,
beating constantly. Using a
metal spoon, fold in cream and
egg whites. Pour into glasses and
chill until set. Decorate before
serving.
Serves 8.

VARIATION
If serving as a cheesecake, make
a crust with 100 g (3 1/2 oz) sweet
biscuit crumbs mixed with 75 g
(2 1/2 oz) melted butter and
45 ml (3 tbsp) chopped, toasted
almonds. Press onto base of a
greased 20 cm (8 in) pie dish and
chill. Use curd cheese instead of
cream cheese for filling, and
decorate with a lattice of
whipped cream, positioning
lychees in squares.

ICE CREAMS

If you do not have an electric ice cream maker, or a churn, you can still make truly luscious ice creams – surely the most popular dessert throughout the world. The Victorians, in fact, treated this ultimate treat with such reverence that they served it with a pointed, serrated spoon so that it could be savoured in ladylike quantities, in the tiniest little scoops, taken on the tip of the tongue. Today, we serve it in bolder quantities, and often nestled on a sauce. The vernacular is pool, or puddle, or swirl, or twirl – all of which fancy rhetoric simply boils down to a drizzle of sauce on a serving plate. Another alternative is to serve several scoops, in different flavours, in a brandy snap basket, or accompanied by a crisp tuile. But however you choose to serve

it, ice cream always makes the perfect ending to a dinner, and the fact that it needs to be made well in advance means that a hostess is free to concentrate on the rest of the meal. The only drawback, to my mind, is that certain recipes require the mixture to be removed from the freezer several times, and re-whipped to ensure a smooth texture. This is a nuisance, and so I usually make ice creams that settle down smoothly in one easy operation, due to the ingredients used. You might have to fold the mixture over, once or twice while setting, but you won't have to remove it from the container to do so. The following are super examples. They are nicely rich and creamy, but do bear in mind that most of them should be allowed to soften for about 5 minutes before serving.

AMARETTO ICE CREAM WITH PURÉED PEARS

A sweet and wickedly rich dessert which is unbelievably easy to make. Preparation time is minimal; ingredients – but for the Amaretto – are basic; and presentation is simple. However, if you have the time, treat your guests to a trio of flavours – this Amaretto ice would go well with the vanilla and mango, while the pear purée will complement all three. Serve in small scoops, on pretty plates, with a ribbon of the purée, add one perfect strawberry, and a slice of kiwi fruit for colour.

3 eggs, separated
100 g (3½ oz) caster sugar
25 ml (5 tsp) Amaretto liqueur
60 g (2 oz) finely chopped,
   toasted almonds (optional)
250 ml (8 fl oz) whipping
   cream, whipped
a few drops of vanilla extract

PEAR PURÉE
400 g (14 oz) canned pears in
   natural juice
1 stick cinnamon
2 whole cloves

Beat egg yolks and sugar very well until thick and pale. Stir in liqueur and almonds, if using. Fold in cream, and egg whites stiffly whisked with a pinch of salt. Finally add vanilla, and fold everything together gently but thoroughly. Pour into a 1.5 litre (2½ pint) container and freeze.

Make purée by putting pears, plus juice and spices, into a small saucepan. Slowly bring to the boil and then boil, uncovered, for a few minutes. Cool. Remove spices and blend until smooth in a blender. Chill, then serve as suggested.
Serves 8.

COFFEE PECAN BRANDY ICE CREAM

This one always elicits a rolling of the eyes. It does not need a sauce, but for variety try nestling a scoop with two other flavours (perhaps vanilla and chocolate) in a lacy brandy-snap basket. If you would rather have a sauce – and it certainly does add eye-appeal – trickle just a little chocolate sauce over the top of each scoop of ice cream, allowing it to run down the sides.

20 ml (4 tsp) pure, instant
  coffee granules
45 ml (3 tbsp) brandy
400 g (14 oz) canned
  condensed milk
a few drops of vanilla extract
500 ml (17 fl oz) whipping
  cream, whipped
4 egg whites
45 g (1 1/2 oz) finely chopped,
  toasted pecan nuts

Dissolve coffee in brandy, then stir into condensed milk. Add vanilla. Fold in cream, then fold in egg whites, stiffly whisked with a pinch of salt. Lastly add nuts. When folding, do so gently but thoroughly – mixture should be a uniform colour, with no streaks. Pour into a 2 litre (3 1/2 pint) freezer container and freeze quickly, folding over once again as it sets.
Makes about 16 large scoops.

LIGHT AND MARBLED CHOCOLATE ICE CREAM

Here is a modest but good alternative to rich and expensive ice creams. Serve plain, or on a small pool of coffee liqueur cream*. The texture of this ice cream is best if made and served on the same day.

3 eggs, separated
200 g (7 oz) caster sugar
400 g (14 oz) canned
  evaporated milk, chilled for
  at least 12 hours
dash of lemon juice
60 ml (4 tbsp) cocoa powder
10 ml (2 tsp) pure, instant
  coffee granules
60 ml (4 tbsp) hot water
a few drops of vanilla extract

Use an electric hand-held mixer and whisk ingredients in following order – then there will be no need to wash beaters in between. Whisk egg whites fairly stiffly, then add sugar very slowly, whisking constantly, until all sugar has been added and mixture is thick and glossy. In a very large mixing bowl, whisk evaporated milk until stiff and trebled in volume, adding lemon juice as you go. Dissolve cocoa powder and coffee in hot water. Beat egg yolks very well and then beat in cocoa-coffee mixture. Now, using a metal spoon, fold everything together, including vanilla, scraping from the bottom of the bowl until an attractive marbled effect is achieved – do not overmix. Pour into a 2.5 litre (4 1/2 pint) container and freeze.
Serves 8–10.

* A straightforward mixture of softly whipped cream and coffee liqueur. The proportions are 250 ml (8 fl oz) whipping cream to 25 ml (5 tsp) liqueur. Prepare just before serving.

Adding a little vanilla essence to desserts containing uncooked egg yolks helps to dissipate any raw aftertaste. A better method is to use vanilla sugar. Tuck a vanilla pod or two into a jar of sugar, and leave to impart its inimitable flavour.

VANILLA ICE CREAM WITH PAWPAW COULIS

This is a basic recipe for a quick-to-make vanilla ice cream. Instead of the ubiquitous chocolate sauce, try the refreshing coulis instead. Serve a scoop of ice cream nestled on a pool of coulis.

ICE CREAM
4 egg whites
500 ml (17 fl oz) whipping cream
400 g (14 oz) canned condensed milk
vanilla extract to flavour

Whisk egg whites stiffly with a good pinch of salt. Add cream and whip again until stiff. Add condensed milk and vanilla and whip well. Turn into a 2 litre (3 ½ pint) freezer container and freeze quickly.
Makes about 12 large scoops.

PAWPAW COULIS WITH RUM OR GINGER

A sweet coulis is simply a purée of fruit, either canned, stewed or fresh. The latter is the nicest, with its tangy flavour off-setting the sweet, rich ice cream. Pour the coulis onto the serving plates, dip a skewer in thick cream and carefully draw it through the purée to form a cobwebby pattern.

250 g (9 oz) peeled, sweet, ripe pawpaw (peeled weight)
200 ml (7 fl oz) fresh orange juice
30 ml (2 tbsp) pale, thin honey*
1 small knob preserved ginger or 10 ml (2 tsp) dark rum (or to taste)
a few drops of lemon juice

Dice pawpaw, place in a blender goblet and blend with orange

juice, honey and ginger, if using, until absolutely smooth. Pour into a jug, then mix in rum, if using, and lemon juice. Do not chill or it will be too thick to pour around ice cream.
Makes about 500 ml (17 fl oz).

* For a stronger flavour, substitute 5 ml (1 tsp) ginger syrup for 5 ml (1 tsp) of the honey.

ITALIAN MERINGUE ICE CREAM WITH ALMONDS

This snowy ice cream is made with a sugar syrup. This requires a little care in the making, but if you have ever boiled fudge, you will know what a soft-ball stage is and should therefore have no problem. It is a fluffy, soft ice cream and makes a spectacular dessert served in scoops on a pool of Strawberry Purée (see box alongside).

125 ml (4 fl oz) water
200 g (7 oz) sugar
6 egg whites
125 ml (4 fl oz) whipping cream
125 ml (4 fl oz) cultured soured cream
a few drops of vanilla extract
45 ml (3 tbsp) sweet sherry
75 g (2 ½ oz) chopped, toasted almonds

Place water and sugar in a small saucepan and slowly bring to boil, stirring to dissolve sugar. Sugar must have dissolved by the time mixture comes to the boil. Boil rapidly, without stirring, for 3–5 minutes until mixture, when tested, will drop from spoon in a long syrupy thread, and a drop will form a soft ball when plopped into a saucer of cold water. Do not boil past this stage as you will end up with a caramel syrup. Keep warm.

In a large bowl, whisk egg whites stiffly with a pinch of salt. Slowly pour sugar syrup

onto whites in a steady stream, whisking constantly. You will need an electric mixer for this. When mixture becomes a stiff and glossy meringue, place bowl in refrigerator for 45 minutes. Whip together cream, soured cream and vanilla until thick. Add sherry and whip again. Fold cream mixture into meringue, together with the almonds. Pour into a 2 litre (3½ pint) container and freeze quickly.
Serves 8.

STRAWBERRY PURÉE
250 g (9 oz) strawberries, hulled, rinsed and sliced
30 ml (2 tbsp) caster sugar

Put strawberries into blender and stand for about 30 minutes to draw the juices. Blend until smooth, then sieve.

MANGO ICE CREAM

A variation on the plain vanilla theme, this is surely the nicest of fruit ice creams. The mango flavour is so delicate that the ice cream is best served without any sauce to mask the flavour.

1 recipe for Vanilla Ice Cream (page 116)
1 kg (2¼ lb) ripe, fibreless mangoes (unpeeled weight)

Peel and slice mangoes and purée in a blender until smooth. You should have about 500 ml (17 fl oz) pulp. Make ice cream according to directions and after adding vanilla, fold in mango pulp gently but thoroughly, then freeze. For finest flavour and texture, serve after a few hours, when just firm.
Makes about 2.25 litres (4 pints).

FROZEN CHRISTMAS PUDDING

A fruity, nutty ice cream, lightly laced with rum. It makes a nice alternative to hot Christmas pudding. Allow ice cream to soften slightly before serving.

125 g (4 oz) mixed, dried fruit
12 glacé cherries, chopped
2 preserved figs, chopped
1 knob preserved ginger, chopped
45 ml (3 tbsp) dark rum
375 ml (13 fl oz) milk
3 eggs, separated
75 g (2½ oz) caster sugar
25 ml (5 tsp) honey
60 g (2 oz) chopped walnuts or pecan nuts
a few drops of vanilla extract
250 ml (8 fl oz) chilled whipping cream, whipped
extra whipped cream to decorate

Mix fruit and ginger in a soup plate, pour rum over; leave to macerate overnight. Scald milk. Beat egg yolks with sugar and honey. Pour scalded milk onto beaten egg mixture, then return mixture to saucepan and cook over low heat, stirring, until it thickens and coats back of spoon. Pour into a bowl, cool, and chill. Add fruit, nuts and vanilla; fold in cream and stiffly whisked egg whites. (Both cream and custard must be very cold, so that fruit does not plummet to the bottom.) Pour into a 1.5–2 litre (2½–3 pint) freezer container, lined with two thick strips of foil, long enough to overlap the edges, for easier unmoulding, and freeze overnight. Turn out and decorate.
Serves 8.

STRAWBERRY SORBET

The colour of this fruity sorbet is quite dramatic, and the inclusion of the honey and egg whites makes a slightly softer mixture, which many people seem to prefer.

125 ml (4 fl oz) **fresh orange juice**
500 g (18 oz) **ripe strawberries, hulled, rinsed and sliced**
45 ml (3 tbsp) **each caster sugar and pale, thin honey**
2 egg whites, **stiffly whisked**

Combine orange juice, strawberries, sugar and honey and leave to stand for about 20 minutes. Place in a blender goblet and blend well, then sieve into a shallow freezer container, pushing through with the back of a spoon. (Using a shallow rather than a deep container allows for quick freezing.) Freeze until solid, then remove, leave to soften slightly, then spoon into bowl of a food processor fitted with grinding blade and process to a slush, stopping occasionally to scrape down sides. Spoon into a mixing bowl and, using a metal spoon, fold in egg whites. Refreeze.
Makes about 24 small scoops.

PEACH, PASSION-FRUIT AND YOGHURT SHERBET

400 g (14 oz) **canned peach slices, drained, syrup reserved**
25 ml (5 tsp) **pale, thin honey**
250 ml (8 fl oz) **plain, thick Bulgarian yoghurt**
125 g (4 oz) **canned sweetened passionfruit pulp**
2 egg whites, **stiffly whisked**

Place peaches in blender goblet with 100 ml (3 1/2 fl oz) of syrup, honey and yoghurt. Blend to a smooth purée. Turn into shallow freezer container; freeze solid. Remove from freezer and stand until beginning to soften. Place scoops into a food processor fitted with grinding blade. Process to a mush. Turn into a bowl, fold in passionfruit pulp and egg whites, and re-freeze.
Makes about 1.5 litres (2 1/2 pints).

SWEETMELON AND GINGER SORBET

500 g (18 oz) **peeled sweetmelon, diced (peeled weight)**
1 **walnut-sized knob preserved ginger**
45 ml (3 tbsp) **caster sugar**
25 ml (5 tsp) **ginger syrup**
125 ml (4 fl oz) **water**
2 egg whites, **stiffly whisked**

Place melon in a blender goblet with ginger, sugar, syrup and water. Blend to a thick, smooth purée. Turn into a shallow freezer container and freeze solid. Turn into a food processor fitted with grinding blade, and process to a soft mush. Spoon into a large bowl and, using a metal spoon, fold in egg whites, then refreeze until solid. Soften slightly before serving in small scoops.
Makes about 16 scoops.

PEAR AND CINNAMON SORBET

A creamy white dessert sorbet, spiked with cinnamon, and quite delicious. Colour-wise, it makes a perfect foil for the bright strawberry and sweet melon sorbets, or pile small scoops into the hollows of canned pear halves for a refreshing, fruity dessert.

250 ml (8 fl oz) water
75 g (2¹/₂ oz) caster sugar
25 ml (5 tsp) pale, thin honey
2 sticks cinnamon
15 ml (1 tbsp) lemon juice
675–750 g (1¹/₂–1³/₄ lb) ripe but unblemished dessert pears, peeled and sliced
2 egg whites

Place water, sugar, honey, cinnamon and lemon juice in a saucepan, bring to the boil, stirring to dissolve sugar, then simmer, covered, for a few minutes. Add pears and simmer, covered, for about 10 minutes until very soft. Cool. Remove cinnamon sticks, then purée mixture in a blender until smooth. Turn into a shallow container and freeze solid – this will take several hours. Remove from freezer and stand until just soft enough to be spooned. Place scoops in a food processor fitted with grinding blade, add unbeaten egg whites one by one, and process until fluffy and smooth. You will probably have to stop machine now and then to break up the bigger chunks. When ready, mixture will look rather like slightly granular, thick white snow. Turn into container and freeze again until solid. Serve within a few days of making.
Makes about 1 litre (1³/₄ pints).

TIPSY FRUIT BAVAROIS

Set in a rounded mould, decorate with cream and a sprig of holly, and serve as a cold alternative to a Christmas pudding.

250 g (9 oz) mixed dried fruit
12 glacé cherries, chopped
2 walnut-sized knobs preserved ginger, finely chopped
125 ml (4 fl oz) sweet sherry
20 ml (4 tsp) gelatine
45 ml (3 tbsp) cold water
500 ml (17 fl oz) milk
4 eggs, separated
75 g (2¹/₂ oz) caster sugar
a few drops of vanilla extract
250 ml (8 fl oz) whipping cream, whipped with
10 ml (2 tsp) dark rum
slightly sweetened whipped cream to decorate

Mix dried fruit, cherries and ginger in a shallow bowl. Pour sherry over, cover, and macerate overnight. Sponge gelatine in water. Scald milk. Beat egg yolks with sugar. Pour on hot milk, return to saucepan and cook, stirring, until mixture coats back of a spoon – do not boil. Remove from hob and stir in gelatine. When dissolved, add vanilla, pour into a large mixing bowl, cool, and then chill until just beginning to set. (This is important as if you add fruit too soon, it will sink to the bottom.) Stir in macerated fruit. Using a metal spoon fold in rum-flavoured cream, and then egg whites, whisked with a pinch of salt. Pour into a rinsed mould and refrigerate until set.

To unmould, run a flat-bladed knife round the edges, and turn out onto a serving platter. Despite texture being beautifully light and fluffy, dessert should unmould easily. Decorate just before serving.
Serves 8–10.

FRUIT SALAD WITH SUGAR-CREAM TOPPING (1)

A medley of fresh fruit topped with yoghurt and cream, drizzled with soft brown sugar and chilled until the sugar melts to a runny, slightly crunchy toffee. There are many versions of this nouvelle fruit salad, but the following is, to my mind, quite the simplest and best. The fruit is not sprinkled with either sugar or alcohol, and so you are not left with a pool of juices at the bottom of the bowl. (However, if you must have a little kick, use just a tiny tot of liqueur.) The topping is ultra-quick – I find there is no need to drain the yoghurt before using, as long as you use the thick, unflavoured Bulgarian yoghurt. The fruit may be varied according to season but the following is an excellent basic combination. The topping is enough for about 1 kg (2¼ lb) fruit.

400 g (14 oz) peeled pawpaw (peeled weight)
400 g (14 oz) peeled sweet melon (peeled weight)
1 large Golden Delicious apple
pulp of 4 passionfruit

TOPPING
250 ml (8 fl oz) thick Bulgarian yoghurt
250 ml (8 fl oz) whipping cream, stiffly whipped
125 g (4 oz) soft dark brown sugar*

Dice pawpaw and melon. Peel apple, dice and toss in a little lemon juice. Mix prepared fruits with passionfruit pulp in a glass serving bowl – use a deep, rather than a wide bowl, so that cream layer will cover fruit thickly and completely.
To make topping, fold yoghurt into cream and spread over fruit. Sprinkle evenly with sugar and then chill, uncovered, for 4–5 hours, by which time sugar will have started to melt and trickle down through cream. Dessert should be served at this stage – if left too long, colour of topping will dissipate and salad will become watery.
Serves 8.

* Be sure to use moist, dark brown sugar – the kind which packs so firmly into a measuring cup that you have to turn it into the palm of your hand and sprinkle it on with your fingers.

FRUIT SALAD WITH SUGAR-CREAM TOPPING (2)

In this recipe bananas and pears (which are good choices because they do not weep), are folded into an orange-flavoured cream. For special occasions replace the brown sugar topping with a sprinkling of caramelised orange zest.

4 ripe, firm bananas, thinly sliced
4 medium, ripe but unbruised pears, peeled and cubed
25 ml (5 tsp) lemon juice
25 ml (5 tsp) pale, thin honey
125 ml (4 fl oz) whipping cream
2.5 ml (½ tsp) very finely grated orange rind
25 ml (5 tsp) orange-flavoured liqueur
100 ml (3½ fl oz) thick Bulgarian yoghurt
orange zest or 25 ml (5 tsp) soft brown sugar for topping

Place fruit in a glass bowl and toss with lemon juice and honey. Whip cream with orange rind and liqueur until stiff – this will take longer than usual, because of the liqueur, but a good quality cream will thicken. Gently fold in yoghurt, then fold cream into fruit. Sprinkle with topping and chill, uncovered, for 3–4 hours.
Serves 6–8.

LEMON CHEESECAKE (1)

Although cheesecakes, these days, come in a wide spectrum of flavours and all the colours of the rainbow, lemon cheesecake is still the one favoured by most fans. The following time-worn version is particularly quick and easy. As the condensed milk makes it pretty rich, I have used low-fat curd instead of cream cheese, and soured cream instead of double with excellent results – the cheesecake remains smooth and creamy, but has a refreshing tang.

CRUMB CRUST
150 g (5 oz) biscuit crumbs
100 g (3¹/₂ oz) melted butter
60 ml (4 tbsp) desiccated coconut

FILLING
15 ml (1 tbsp) gelatine
45 ml (3 tbsp) water
400 g (14 oz) canned condensed milk
250 g (9 oz) curd cheese
100 ml (3¹/₂ fl oz) lemon juice
5 ml (1 tsp) very finely grated lemon rind
250 ml (8 fl oz) cultured soured cream
a few drops of vanilla extract
ground cinnamon

Make crust by combining all ingredients. Press onto base of a greased 23 cm (9 in) diameter pie dish and chill.

To make filling, sponge gelatine in cold water and dissolve over low heat. Using an electric mixer, whisk remaining ingredients, except cinnamon, until absolutely smooth. Slowly whisk in slightly cooled gelatine. Pour into crust, dust with cinnamon, and chill until set.
Serves 10–12.

LEMONY YOGHURT CHEESECAKE (2)

A simpler and much lighter alternative, using yoghurt instead of cream, making this a fine choice for those with an eye on the calories. If liked, the crust may be omitted altogether and the filling simply spooned into individual glass bowls, chilled, and served as a light lemon dessert with an optional topping of whipped cream flavoured with a dash of brandy.

COCONUT CRUMB CRUST
100 g (3¹/₂ oz) biscuit crumbs
2.5 ml (¹/₂ tsp) finely grated lemon rind
75 g (2¹/₂ oz) melted butter
75 ml (5 tbsp) desiccated coconut

FILLING
250 g (9 oz) curd cheese
60 ml (4 tbsp) caster sugar
25 ml (5 tsp) pale, thin honey
2 eggs, separated
5 ml (1 tsp) finely grated lemon rind
a few drops of vanilla extract
10 ml (2 tsp) gelatine
45 ml (3 tbsp) lemon juice
250 ml (8 fl oz) thick Bulgarian yoghurt
ground cinnamon for topping

Mix ingredients for crust and line base of greased 20 cm (8 in) pie dish and chill.

To make filling, whisk together curd cheese, sugar, honey, egg yolks, lemon rind and vanilla. Sponge gelatine in lemon juice and dissolve over low heat. Whisk slowly into cheese mixture. Stir in yoghurt, then fold in egg whites, stiffly whisked with a pinch of salt. Pour onto crust, spreading evenly, and dust with cinnamon. Chill until set.
Serves 8.

BAKED CHEESECAKE

PROCESSOR CRUST
75 g (2¹/₂ oz) plain (soft if available) flour
15 ml (1 tbsp) caster sugar
1.25 ml (¹/₄ tsp) baking powder
60 g (2 oz) cold butter, diced
30 ml (1 tbsp) toasted, slivered almonds (optional)

FILLING
500 g (18 oz) curd cheese, or 250 g (9 oz) each cream and curd cheese
25 ml (5 tsp) cornflour
5 ml (1 tsp) very finely grated orange rind
pinch of salt
3 eggs
a few drops of vanilla extract
125 ml (4 fl oz) whipping cream
100 g (3¹/₂ oz) caster sugar
2.5 ml (¹/₂ tsp) ground cinnamon

TOPPING
400 g (14 oz) canned apricot halves, drained, juice reserved
5 ml (1 tsp) cornflour
toasted almonds to decorate

To make crust, place flour, sugar, baking powder and butter in a food processor fitted with grinding blade and process until mixture forms a soft ball. Remove, mix in almonds, if using, and pat onto lightly oiled base of a loose-bottomed, 20 cm diameter x 7.5 cm deep (8 x 3 in deep) tin. Prick well; bake on middle shelf of oven at 180 °C (350 °F, gas 4) for 15 minutes, then cool. Make filling by beating all ingredients together until smooth – Mixture will be runny. Sprinkle 5 ml (1 tsp) caster sugar over base of baked crust, then pour in cheese mixture. Bake on middle shelf of oven at 160 °C (325 °F, gas 3) for 1 hour 10 minutes, or until lightly browned, risen and firm. Turn off oven, leave door ajar, and leave to cool. Remove from oven and remove ring. Arrange apricots, rounded sides up, on top of cheesecake, and glaze by mixing 100 ml (3¹/₂ fl oz) reserved apricot syrup with cornflour. Bring to the boil in a small saucepan, stirring, and boil until thick and clear. Using a pastry brush, paint tops of apricots. Position toasted almonds in between apricots.
Serves 8–10.

ORANGE AND APRICOT CHEESECAKE

Cheesecakes set with gelatine are easier and creamier. Use the above pastry crust, or a biscuit crust.

FILLING
500 g (18 oz) curd cheese
3 eggs, separated
5 ml (1 tsp) finely grated orange rind
a few drops of vanilla extract
140 g (4¹/₂ oz) caster sugar
2.5 ml (¹/₂ tsp) ground cinnamon
25 ml (5 tsp) gelatine
60 ml (4 tbsp) fresh orange juice
250 ml (8 fl oz) whipping cream, softly whipped

Whisk cheese, egg yolks, orange rind, vanilla, sugar and cinnamon together until smooth and thick. Sponge gelatine in orange juice and dissolve over low heat. Slowly whisk into cheese mixture. Using a metal spoon, fold in cream and egg whites whisked with a pinch of salt. Pour onto crust and chill until set. Top with apricots, and glaze and decorate as in previous recipe.
Serves 8–10.

BAKED APPLE AND BANANA PUFF

Sweet and simple, this is an old-fashioned dessert which can be prepared in a flash. The ingredients are basic and inexpensive, with oil replacing butter very successfully. Serve warm, rather than hot, with softly whipped cream, custard or ice cream.

750 g (1³/4 lb) canned unsweetened apple pie filling
2 bananas, thinly sliced
125 g (4 oz) golden syrup
100 ml (3¹/2 fl oz) hot water
60 g (2 oz) seedless raisins or sultanas
125 g (4 oz) self-raising flour
5 ml (1 tsp) ground mixed spice
75 g (2¹/2 oz) light brown sugar
30 g (1 oz) desiccated coconut
250 ml (8 fl oz) sunflower oil
2 eggs
pinch of salt

Chop apples coarsely, add bananas, and spoon into a buttered, deep, 23 cm (9 in) pie dish. Melt syrup in water and pour over. Sprinkle with raisins or sultanas. Whisk remaining ingredients together to make a thick batter. Drop large spoonfuls over fruit – batter will spread during baking. Bake at 180 ˚C (350 ˚F, gas 4) for 35 minutes, until puffy and lightly browned. **Serves 8.**

ORANGE AND CINNAMON TUILES

Tuiles are thin, slightly curved biscuits, usually flavoured with almonds, and hostesses with reputations like to serve them with light desserts or ice creams to add a touch of French flair. Once baked, the tuiles are draped over a rolling pin to cool, to achieve the traditional `roof tile' shape. They are not difficult to make, but can be capricious by refusing to remain crisp. My solution is simply to bake them twice. Voilà!

1 egg white
60 ml (4 tbsp) caster sugar
15 ml (1 tbsp) each plain flour and cornflour
1.25 ml (¹/4 tsp) ground cinnamon
5 ml (1 tsp) very finely grated orange rind
a few drops of vanilla extract
30 g (1 oz) melted butter

Whisk egg white to soft peak stage. Add sugar very slowly, beating constantly to a stiff and glossy meringue. Sift together flour, cornflour and cinnamon. Using a metal spoon, fold into meringue mixture, together with orange rind and vanilla, then fold in melted butter. Combine lightly but thoroughly. Drop large teaspoonfuls of mixture onto a large, lightly oiled baking tray, spacing well apart. (You will need to bake them in batches, making no more than six at a time.) Spread each one out thinly into a 7.5 cm (3 in) circle, using back of spoon and swirling in a circular motion. Bake at 180 ˚C (350 ˚F, gas 4) for about 5 minutes, or until browned round edges. Using a spatula, remove and place over a rolling pin, or an upturned cup, pressing down very lightly to achieve curved shape. Cool, and turn off oven. When tuiles are cold, replace on baking tray and return to cooled oven until golden brown and crisp. It is also possible to re-bake them very briefly before oven has cooled. They will flatten out, and should be shaped again on removing. Store in an airtight tin when cold, adding a sprinkling of sugar to retain crispness. **Makes 12 tuiles.**

FRUIT SALAD WITH FLAIR (1)

Whether taken neat, or dolloped with cream or ice cream, a serving of fresh fruit is the unfailingly pop-ular dénouement to a fine dinner, subtly inferring that the hostess is one who cares for the well-being and waistlines of her guests. Although fruit salad can be the simplest mix of seasonal fruits, layered with a little caster sugar to draw the juices, macerating the fruit in a sugar syrup flavoured with liqueur certainly adds a dash of flair.

The following recipe is a basic guide as to the proportions to use. Comparatively inexpensive maraschino liqueur adds sweetness and a subtle flavour, but feel free to substitute seasonal fruits and other liqueurs, according to preference. Serve with vanilla ice cream, softly whipped cream, or half Bulgarian yoghurt and half whipped cream, folded together.

250 g (9 oz) strawberries, hulled, rinsed and sliced
4 thin slices fresh pineapple, finely diced
400 g (14 oz) peeled pawpaw, diced
2 bananas, thinly sliced and tossed in lemon juice

SYRUP
125 ml (4 fl oz) water
45 ml (3 tbsp) sugar
60 ml (4 tbsp) maraschino liqueur

Place fruit in a glass serving bowl – it should be wide, rather than deep, so that liquid does not only bathe bottom layer of fruit.

Make syrup by heating water and sugar in a small saucepan. Stir until sugar has dissolved, then boil rapidly, uncovered, for 2–3 minutes. Remove from heat; stir in maraschino, then cool.

Pour syrup over fruit, tossing very gently to mix, then cover and refrigerate for a few hours. **Serves 8–10.**

FRUIT SALAD (2)

No time to make a sugar syrup? Simply mix the following superb fruits – Galia melon (which smells like a flower garden), pineapple, fibreless mangoes and passionfruit. Add sugar and rum, and chill. Use the following weights as a rough guide – you can't really go wrong.

Peel and dice enough melon, pineapple and mango to give a total weight of 575 g (1¼ lb). Place in glass dessert bowl and mix in pulp of 4 passionfruit. Sprinkle with 30 ml (2 tbsp) caster sugar and 30 ml (2 tbsp) dark rum (or more if you want a really rummy salad). Cover and refrigerate for several hours or overnight. Serve plain, or with softly whipped cream, crème fraîche (see box, page 38), or ice cream.
Serves 5–6.

WHOLEMEAL AND OAT APPLE CRUMBLE

The sort of dessert you would meet in a vegetarian restaurant. It is important to use Golden Delicious apples – they have just the right texture and sweetness. Serve this wholesome dessert with thick cream or ice cream.

about 750 g (1¾ lb) Golden Delicious apples
375 ml (13 fl oz) water
a nut of butter
30 ml (2 tbsp) pale, thin honey
2 sticks cinnamon
4 whole cloves
45 g (1½ oz) seedless raisins or sultanas

CRUMBLE
45 g (1½ oz) oats
60 g (2 oz) wholemeal flour
75 ml (5 tbsp) light brown sugar
5 ml (1 tsp) ground cinnamon

2.5 ml (¹/2 tsp) mixed ground
  spice or 1.25 ml (¹/4 tsp)
  freshly grated nutmeg
a handful of chopped walnuts
  or pecan nuts
45 g (1¹/2 oz) soft butter

Peel, slice and core apples. Place
in saucepan with water, butter,
honey and spices. Bring to the
boil, then cover and simmer very
gently until soft. Do not overcook, or boil rapidly, as it is
important to retain a generous
quantity of poaching liquid.
Remove cinnamon sticks and
cloves, add raisins or sultanas,
and spoon into a deep, 20 cm
(8 in) pie dish, adding all liquid,
then cool. (If liked, prepare to
this point several hours ahead.)

To make crumble, mix oats,
flour, sugar, spices and nuts. Rub
in butter very well, until you
have a crumbly, moist mixture.
Strew over apples to cover thickly, and bake at 180 ˚C (350 ˚F,
gas 4) for about 35 minutes.
Serves 6.

LEMON SNOW WITH ORANGE CRÈME ANGLAISE

*This light-as-air dessert, tangy with
lemon, is as refreshing as a sorbet
and makes a fine finale to a rich
dinner. The texture is not unlike a
frothy meringue mixture, to which
has been added the minimum
amount of gelatine, making it just
possible to be set in little ramekins
and unmoulded, or simply served in
egg-shaped, soft scoops, using a
tablespoon, and nestled on individual plates. Either way, they are
served with a pool of flavoured custard. Frosted grapes make a pretty
decoration, but when out of season,
use mint leaves.*

LEMON SNOW
60 ml (4 tbsp) water
15 ml (1 tbsp) gelatine
125 ml (4 fl oz) lemon juice
10 ml (2 tsp) very finely grated
  lemon rind

180 g (6 oz) caster sugar
6 egg whites
250 ml (8 fl oz) whipping
  cream, softly whipped

LIGHT ORANGE CRÈME ANGLAISE
500 ml (17 fl oz) milk
finely grated rind of 1 large
  orange
4 egg yolks
30 ml (2 tbsp) caster sugar
10 ml (2 tsp) cornflour
pinch of salt
a few drops of vanilla extract

To make lemon snow, pour
water into small saucepan,
sprinkle on gelatine and sponge
for a minute. Add lemon juice,
rind and sugar, and stir over low
heat until gelatine and sugar
have dissolved. Cool until cold
and syrupy, but not set. Whisk
egg whites with a pinch of salt
until stiff. Very slowly whisk in
cold gelatine mixture – mixture
will slowly take on appearance of
a soft, glossy meringue. Using a
metal spoon, fold in cream

quickly and gently – expect
meringue to deflate just a little.
Turn immediately into a glass
bowl or rinsed ramekins and
refrigerate.

To make crème anglaise, slowly
heat milk and orange rind in a
small saucepan. Whisk together
yolks, sugar, cornflour and salt.
Strain scalded milk onto egg
mixture, then pour into double
boiler and stir over simmering
water until thickened. Add
vanilla, pour into a jug, cool
and chill.

For Frosted Grapes, wash and
dry grapes thoroughly, leaving
stalks attached. Whisk an egg
white until floppy, dip in grapes,
one by one, shake off excess,
then roll each grape in caster
sugar to coat on all sides, and
leave on a plate to dry.
Serves 8–10.

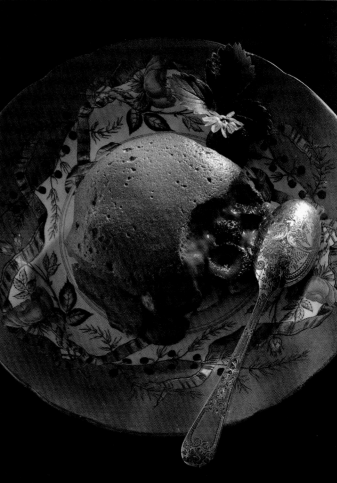

HOT APRICOT SPONGE

60 g (2 oz) soft butter
75 g (2½ oz) caster sugar
5 ml (1 tsp) finely grated
   orange rind
3 eggs, separated
60 ml (4 tbsp) self-raising flour
250 ml (8 fl oz) milk
45 ml (3 tbsp) fresh orange
   juice
25 ml (5 tsp) orange-flavoured
   liqueur
60 ml (4 tbsp) desiccated
   coconut
400 g (14 oz) canned apricot
   halves, drained
ground cinnamon

Cream butter and sugar until
light. Add orange rind and egg
yolks and beat well. Sprinkle
flour over top and fold in. Whisk
together milk, orange juice and
liqueur, and stir into creamed
mixture. Add coconut, and then
fold in egg whites whisked with

a pinch of salt. Butter an oval
25 x 20 cm (10 x 8 in) baking
dish, or a 20 cm (8 in) square,
and arrange apricots, rounded
sides up, on base – they will not
cover it completely. Pour batter
over and sprinkle with cinnamon. Place dish in a large baking
tin with hot water to reach halfway up sides. Bake at 160 °C
(325 °F, gas 3) for about 45 minutes, until browned and set.
Serves 6–8.

CHOCOLATE, ORANGE AND STRAWBERRY DESSERT

*A sinfully rich dessert: liqueur-
soaked biscuits, fresh strawberries,
and a silky chocolate mousse which
sensible men will stoutly refuse
while women will relish it even
while complaining about their hips.*

125 ml (4 fl oz) fresh orange
   juice
45 ml (3 tbsp) orange-
   flavoured liqueur
125 g (4 oz) sponge finger
   (boudoir) biscuits
200 g (7 oz) fresh strawberries,
   hulled, rinsed, dried and
   thinly sliced
milled black pepper
100 g (3½ oz) each plain
   chocolate and milk chocolate
   (not white)
45 ml (3 tbsp) water
10 ml (2 tsp) pure, instant
   coffee granules
45–60 g (1½–2 oz) butter
6 eggs, separated
250 ml (8 fl oz) cream whipped
   with a few drops of vanilla
   extract
strawberries to decorate

Mix orange juice and liqueur in
a large soup plate, and soak biscuits – do this in relays, and turn
them over once or twice to
moisten thoroughly. Arrange in
a single layer on base of a large

rectangular or 23 cm (9 in)
square serving dish. You might
have to break them to fit, and by
the time you have soaked them
all, the juice should have been
absorbed. Arrange strawberries
on top of biscuits. Grind over a
little black pepper. Break up
chocolate and put into top of
double boiler with water and coffee. Melt over gently simmering
water. Add butter and stir until
melted and mixture is smooth.
Cool for about 5 minutes, then
slowly stir in beaten egg yolks.
Turn into a mixing bowl, and,
using a metal spoon, fold in
cream. Whisk egg whites with a
pinch of salt, stir a few spoonfuls
through chocolate mixture, then
fold in remainder. Combine gently but thoroughly, and then
pour in an even layer over strawberries. Refrigerate overnight.
Decorate with a cluster of berries
before serving.
Serves 10-12.

INDEX